# The Money Savvy Teen

# The Money Savvy Teen

## Building Smart Financial Habits That Will Last a Lifetime

*Robbie Hyman*

BLOOMSBURY ACADEMIC
NEW YORK • LONDON • OXFORD • NEW DELHI • SYDNEY

BLOOMSBURY ACADEMIC
Bloomsbury Publishing Inc, 1359 Broadway, New York, NY 10018, USA
Bloomsbury Publishing Plc, 50 Bedford Square, London, WC1B 3DP, UK
Bloomsbury Publishing Ireland, 29 Earlsfort Terrace, Dublin 2, D02 AY28, Ireland

BLOOMSBURY, BLOOMSBURY ACADEMIC and the Diana logo are trademarks of
Bloomsbury Publishing Plc

First published in the United States of America 2026

Copyright © Robbie Hyman, 2026

Cover design: Jen Huppert
Cover image: © istock/wenjin chen

All rights reserved. No part of this publication may be: i) reproduced or transmitted in any form, electronic or mechanical, including photocopying, recording or by means of any information storage or retrieval system without prior permission in writing from the publishers; or ii) used or reproduced in any way for the training, development or operation of artificial intelligence (AI) technologies, including generative AI technologies. The rights holders expressly reserve this publication from the text and data mining exception as per Article 4(3) of the Digital Single Market Directive (EU) 2019/790.

Bloomsbury Publishing Inc does not have any control over, or responsibility for, any third-party websites referred to or in this book. All internet addresses given in this book were correct at the time of going to press. The author and publisher regret any inconvenience caused if addresses have changed or sites have ceased to exist, but can accept no responsibility for any such changes.

Library of Congress Cataloging-in-Publication Data
Names: Hyman, Robbie author
Title: The money savvy teen : building smart financial habits that will last a lifetime / Robbie Hyman.
Description: New York : Bloomsbury Academic, 2026. | Includes bibliographical references and index. | Audience: Ages 12-22 | Audience: Grades 10-12
Identifiers: LCCN 2025030524 (print) | LCCN 2025030525 (ebook) | ISBN 9798765189122 hardback | ISBN 9798765189146 pdf | ISBN 9798765189139 epub
Subjects: LCSH: Teenagers--Finance, Personal | Young adults--Finance, Personal
Classification: LCC HG179 .H96 2026 (print) | LCC HG179 (ebook)
LC record available at https://lccn.loc.gov/2025030524
LC ebook record available at https://lccn.loc.gov/2025030525

ISBN: HB: 979-8-7651-8912-2
ePDF: 979-8-7651-8914-6
eBook: 979-8-7651-8913-9

Typeset by Deanta Global Publishing Services, Chennai, India
Printed and bound in the United States of America

For product safety related questions contact productsafety@bloomsbury.com.

To find out more about our authors and books visit www.bloomsbury.com and sign up for our newsletters.

# Contents

*Foreword* vii

**Introduction** 1

**PART I  Developing a Healthy Relationship with Money** 9
1   Know Your Whole Money Picture  11
2   Protect Monday Me  19
3   Avoid the Spending Rip Current  25
4   Don't Buy Tomorrow's Junk  33
5   Dodge the Ad Barrage  41
6   Take an Aerial View of Your Finances  49
7   Gamify Your Money Habits  57

**PART II  Getting to Know Your Money Toolkit**  63
8   Checking Accounts  65
9   Savings Accounts  73
10  Credit Cards  81
11  Credit Scores  91
12  Debit Cards  99

13  Bills  105
14  Budgets  111
15  Investments  119

**PART III  Navigating the Social Side of Money  135**
17  Develop a Lending Policy  137
18  Be Careful Borrowing Money  143
19  Watch Out for Peer Pressure  147
20  Create a Giving Plan  151
21  Remind Yourself that Money Isn't a Competition  157
22  Slay the Green-Eyed Monster  167
23  Keep the Details of Your Money Situation to Yourself  171
24  Don't Pretend You Have More Than You Do  177
25  Remember That Other People's Money Is Other People's Money  181
26  Never Feel Guilty About Having Money  187
27  Parting Thoughts  191

*Notes  195*
*Suggested Reading  207*
*Index  209*
*About the Author  214*

# *Foreword*

As a financial planner and author, I see firsthand how critical it is to learn about money at a young age. So many of my clients tell me, "I just don't understand money." And why would they? As of March 2025, only twenty-seven states require financial education in high school. While this is a major improvement from previous years, all this tells me is that almost half of our teens are not being taught about finance. At eighteen years old, teens are thrust out into a world where every step they take from graduation to retirement will be directly impacted by their financial knowledge and money management skills. Career decisions, buying your first house, getting married, having children—finances all play a massive role in each of these life events. And it's not just the major ones; finance is a part of our everyday life. Whether it's where we eat, what we buy, traveling, going out with friends, or negotiating prices, every day we are faced with financial decisions.

Enter *The Money Savvy Teen: Building Smart Financial Habits That Will Last a Lifetime* by Robbie Hyman. Hyman does the impossible (trust me, I try every day). He makes confusing and often dry financial concepts relatable, simple to understand, and fun. I actually laughed out loud several times, which is rare in my line of work. In my personal favorite, Chapter 4, "Don't Buy Tomorrow's Junk," Hyman illustrates the lifecycle of the "unused treadmill," which eventually becomes a really expensive clothes hanger. Too close to home.

What makes this book work so well is that Hyman gets teenagers. As a mother to one—that's an impressive feat. He understands what's important to them, their day-to-day lives, and the struggles they face. This leads to a practical and relatable guide that doesn't just provide what they should do, but *how to do it*. Each chapter includes easy-to-use "life hacks" that allow teens to practice what they learn. An example that I'm going to recommend to my kids comes from Hyman's chapter on the *Societal Side of Money*. When dealing with peer pressure around spending, he recommends coming up with a standard phrase, like "I'm watching my money for a while." Genius, and we could all use one of these one-liners.

Not only does he understand his audience, but breaks down the fundamentals of finance brilliantly. From the very beginning, he emphasizes the importance of understanding the whole money picture first, so you can then evaluate individual decisions. He refers to it as an "Aerial View" of your finances. As a financial planner, I can't emphasize this enough, and it's one of the first concepts I discuss with clients.

The fundamentals include practical information that's critical to being financially healthy around checking accounts, savings accounts, and credit cards. Just having this base knowledge as a teen can dramatically improve their financial health as an adult. He makes lessons that most see as painful (paying bills and budgeting) relatable and manageable.

And while some finance books can feel like a list of warnings and "What not to do," Hyman sends a positive message about money. I highly recommend this book for any teen who wants to learn how to manage their financial world in a responsible way that allows them to enjoy their life and prepare for the future.

*Liz Frazier Peck*
*Certified Financial Planner, Forbes Contributor, and Author of*
Beyond Piggy Banks: How to Teach Young Kids About Finance

# *Introduction*

My brother David had an interesting first day of college. Walking across campus toward class, he passed a row of popup booths that businesses had set up along the walkway. David explained the scene to me: "The most aggressive salespeople that day, the ones who jumped out to block your path, were at the booths offering credit cards."

One of those sales reps stopped my brother and handed him a T-shirt with the credit card company's logo on it. Then he said he could pretty much guarantee that David would qualify for a credit card with a spending limit of at least a few hundred dollars.

Sounds great, right? David thought so. He filled out the application, took his new shirt, and headed to class. (He can't remember for sure, but he thinks the rep also gave him a free coffee mug.) As promised, a few days later a credit card with David's name on it showed up in the mail. Also as promised, the card gave him a several-hundred-dollar spending limit.

Let's stop there. I'm guessing that little anecdote didn't strike you as the beginning of a common financial horror story that can lead to years of money struggles, massive stress, and major setbacks in life. Thankfully, that didn't happen to my brother. But for millions of young people every year, simple encounters like that—*Apply for a credit card; get your free T-shirt!*—begin a long-term nightmare of financial problems that can negatively affect every area of a person's life.

A 2024 study found that the average member of Generation Z (people in their teens and twenties at the time) owed $3,266 on their credit cards.[1] As the report pointed out, this generation was "just getting started on their financial journeys," so it's worth trying to figure out how these young people could have already dug themselves into a hole thousands of dollars deep. Another important question is how those Gen Zers will climb out of that hole and pay back all that debt. The unfortunate answer for many of them: very slowly and very expensively.

And considering how easy it is for young people to rack up serious debt, let's go back to my brother at the credit card booth. Can you think of any important information missing from the conversation he had with the sales rep?

We'll get into the details of credit cards in Chapter 10, but for now you can think of them as portable, on-demand loans you carry around in your wallet or purse. When you use the card to buy something—a meal at a restaurant, a jacket on Amazon—the credit card company actually pays for you. That's the loan part. The repayment part comes about a month later, when the card company sends you a notice to pay back the money they've lent you (or at least a portion of it).

So you'd think the sales rep would want to know if my brother had the ability to repay whatever money he'd be borrowing on the credit card. Some obvious questions he could've asked: *Tell me, David, do you have a lot of savings in the bank?* (He had hardly any.) *A job or other source of income?* (Nope.) *Rich parents who can help if you spend more than you can pay us back?* (Not even close.)

But the rep didn't ask for any of that information. He didn't even ask if David understood what it meant to pay for something using a credit card or how interest rates work. The only question David remembers the rep asking was if the T-shirt was the right size for him.

## Personal-Finance Tools Often Aren't What You Think They Are

There's an old joke: did you hear about the two idiot bankers? After lending out all their money, they skipped town.

Cute line, but it also highlights something you need to understand about credit cards and other forms of lending. You might already be asking yourself this question: why would these companies be so eager to loan their money without first making sure each borrower could pay them back? Are these credit card executives just a bunch of idiot bankers? Short answer: no.

As for the longer answer, this brings us to one of many not-so-obvious truths about personal finance. Credit card companies don't want you to pay them back in full each month. The biggest portion of their profits comes from *interest*: money they charge you for every dollar you borrow but delay repaying beyond the next bill. That's why these companies let you pay just a small percentage of your *balance* (the total you owe) each month. The *minimum payment* they require might be as little as 1 percent or 2 percent of the full amount. For the 98 percent you don't repay by the bill's due date, the credit card company starts charging you interest.

If you become one of those Gen Z cardholders who gets a bill showing a $3,266 balance, you'll also find some "good" news. The bill will tell you, *No rush. You can pay us just, oh, let's say $60 this month.* That might make you feel relieved in the moment, because it means you don't need to come up with thousands of dollars all at once. But here's the problem. The following month, even if you haven't spent another dollar using your credit card, your balance will have grown anyway, because now you also owe *interest* (the price of borrowing money) for not paying off your entire balance last month. When he started using that first card, my brother didn't know any of this.

You might think of a credit card as a tool of convenience. And if you handle it responsibly, that's exactly what it can be for you. But that's not how the credit card companies view these products. They see their cards as tools to help you dig yourself into debt and stay there for years or even decades. That earns them billions.

## We Don't Teach Smart Money Habits to Young People

But we're getting ahead of ourselves. The credit card problem I'm describing is just one symptom of a broader, society-wide ailment. Most people never receive any formal training or education in basic money management—and it shows. People of all ages and income levels regularly make all sorts of avoidable mistakes with their money. The consequences of these missteps can range from annoying inconveniences to serious setbacks to all-out financial ruin. Consider these worrisome money-management facts:

- Americans in 2023 paid more than $5.8 billion to banks in *overdraft charges*.[2] That means they tried to use their bank accounts to pay for stuff that cost more money than they had in their accounts at the time. Banks hit you with hefty penalties for that screwup.

- More than one in three Americans have been charged a *late fee* in the previous twelve months for paying a bill after its due date. This includes bills for credit cards, utilities (phone, electricity, water, etc.), and even rent.[3]

- Nearly 40 percent of Americans say they couldn't come up with the money to pay for a $400 emergency, such as unexpected car trouble or a medical expense.[4] In other words, tens of millions of American adults live day-to-day with so little financial breathing room that even a minor expense could cause them serious problems.

Unfortunately, most schools don't teach personal finance concepts or how to develop smart money habits. And because your parents didn't receive formal education in the subject themselves, they often lack the vocabulary to pass on the money-management wisdom life has taught them. Your mom or dad might give you the general advice: "Don't overspend." "Careful with the impulse purchases." "Just because your friends are buying something." (And yes, we all get these exact same sayings from the parenting manual.)

I'm a dad myself, and my teenage daughter rolled her eyes through a thousand lectures like that. Did my statements have any positive effect on her approach to personal finance? Maybe, maybe not. But if they didn't, if my advice simply went in one eye and rolled out the other (you know what I mean), I can think of at least one reason. I never told her how.

When parents, grandparents, educators, and other adults offer money-management advice to young people, we usually describe only the goal, the outcome. We fail to give you practical guidance or outline any of the steps that could help you get there. We mean well, but to you, it probably sounds like we're just barking orders.

- **"Don't buy stuff you don't need."**
  Great suggestion. But how? What strategies should you use to resist the temptations you'll find everywhere to make impulse purchases?

- "Don't compare what you have to what other people have."
  Okay, but *how*?
- "Watch out for advertisers' tricks, and make sure you're buying things only for the right reasons."
  *How*?
- "Be careful about lending money."
  [After eye roll]: *How*?
- "Don't overspend."
  *How*?!

This book is your answer to how.

# What We'll Cover in This Book

I've broken *The Money Savvy Teen* into three I-promise-they're-not-boring parts, each covering personal finance from a different angle.

## Part I: Developing a Healthy Relationship With Money

Here you'll learn some unique concepts about smart money management, like how to Protect Monday Me and how to Avoid the Spending Rip Current. You'll also get a peek behind the curtain of the advertising game to learn some of the sophisticated tactics they've devised to get into your head and use emotional triggers to sell you stuff. Oh, and we'll pick up some insights from the real-life stories of celebrities who earned millions and then went broke.

## Part II: Getting to Know Your Money Toolkit

We moderns no longer pay for stuff using gold, salt, or feathers (yep, all used as money at one time or another). You'll have a difficult time adulting without savings and checking accounts, credit cards, debit cards, and a few other standard tools that help you keep your financial house running smoothly. So in this part, you'll get to know these components of what I call your Money Toolkit, discover some tips to get the most benefit from these tools, and learn how to avoid their common, costly pitfalls.

## Part III: Navigating the Social Side of Money

The people in our lives (not to mention the ones we know only through social media) often have a massive influence on how we handle and even feel about our money. So the final part will help you build proactive strategies for navigating the social aspects of your financial life. That includes dealing with the big emotions relating to money, like jealousy and guilt, as well as developing strategies to handle the smaller issues, like a friend who asks to borrow some cash.

I've included with every lesson some reader-friendly "hows." These are the easy-to-grasp life hacks I wish I had thought of when my daughter was younger—sorry, Zoe—so I could've avoided having to read her those annoying "Don't overspend" lines straight from the parenting manual. (Okay, I'm kidding. The manual doesn't exist. And speaking for every parent who's ever lived, that's too bad.)

## We're Counting on You

So yeah, from a personal-finance perspective, modern-day America is a hot mess. That's the bad news. But there's great news, too, because here we are.

Look at you now. You're starting a book about smart money management. If I've done my job, you'll come away from this read with at least a few strategies and life hacks that will help you on your journey to becoming a personal-finance powerhouse. And if some of these lessons create lightbulb moments for you, maybe you'll share those insights with friends and help them follow your lead, so they can become money-savvy adults themselves. That just might give us a chance to slowly undo this mess.

It all starts now, with you. Let's go.

*Part I*

# Developing a Healthy Relationship with Money

# 1

# *Know Your Whole Money Picture*

I'll bet you don't know these two facts about movie star Will Smith. First, he was a standout student in high school. Strong grades. Real talent in the sciences. Excellent SAT scores. When his parents sent an application on his behalf to the Milwaukee School of Engineering, the university accepted him immediately.[1] But this young man had no plans to attend college, because he wanted to pursue a music career.

He didn't waste any time. Still in high school, Smith and his friend Jeff Townes formed the hip-hop duo DJ Jazzy Jeff and the Fresh Prince, which quickly became one of the music industry's most successful acts. Within a few years, the group sold more than five million albums. While still in his teens, Smith stacked up a fortune estimated at $10 million.[2] Which brings us to the next fact you probably don't know.

By the time he was in his early twenties, Will Smith had gone broke. Worse than broke, in fact, because he owed the IRS $2.8 million in unpaid taxes.[3]

You can't question young Will Smith's discipline. Nobody builds a chart-topping, multiplatinum music group by being lazy. Smith wasn't a dummy, either, as his grades and SAT scores make clear. So what happened here? And what can it teach you?

Smith fell into the common trap of failing to keep a watchful eye on what I call your Whole Money Picture. The idea is to step back regularly and examine your total financial situation. For the process to work, you need to monitor everything: how much money you have and where it is (in a bank, under your mattress), how much you expect to come in (from a job, gifts, allowance), how much you're spending (on food, clothes, entertainment), and what, if any, financial obligations you have (bills, paying back a loan). Only after you've taken this wide-angle view of your entire financial situation can you make informed decisions about whether you can really afford to buy something.

---

**You need to understand your Whole Money Picture before you can make an intelligent decision about whether any specific purchase is a good idea.**

---

## Shall We Play a Game?

Imagine a young man in high school. Riding his bike home one afternoon, he stops at a shopping center to get an energy drink from the convenience store. He does this every day. But today, he also pops into the game shop and buys a game for his PlayStation. Question: is he spending his money responsibly?

The answer, of course, is that you can't give me a good answer. You don't have enough information. So let me add one more piece of data that might help you. Imagine he hasn't bought a PlayStation game in many months. Now would you say he's spending his money responsibly?

Okay, that was a trick question. The second piece of information doesn't clarify much, does it? You still can't know whether buying the game could put this guy in a bad financial situation. That's because I haven't told you about his Whole Money Picture.

Maybe he has a job and saves most of what he earns. Once in a while, on a day like today, he stops at the game store. He's always aware of his Whole Money Picture and sets aside a little extra for purchases like this when he's comfortable that he has enough money stashed away. In that case, sure, he should buy a game if he wants one. Doing so won't hurt him.

But maybe he has no job, receives very little money from any source, and immediately spends every dollar he gets his hands on. True, he hasn't bought a *video game* in months, but maybe he's recently bought a skateboard, lots of movie tickets, and a pricey new gaming chair. Maybe the cash he's using to buy this game is money his mom gave him to pay for lunches at school. If that's his situation, buying a game could mean he literally goes hungry.

When you understand the Whole Money Picture concept, you can see where young Will Smith went wrong. Remember, Smith was a super-smart teenager. The analytical, mathematical side of his brain definitely would've understood the problem. If you start with even a large amount of money—say, $10 million—subtracting over and over from that number will take it from large to smaller to very small and eventually to $0. You can go broke even after you've gotten rich. It'll just take longer.

The crazy thing is that Smith probably didn't even realize what he was doing, at least not consciously. Raj Patel, MD, a pediatrician with Gila River Health Care in Arizona, told me something interesting: "Our brain can come up with all sorts of creative ways to give us permission to do things we'd like when we know they're bad for us. For example, we can convince ourselves we're doing less of some unhealthy thing than we really are by breaking that behavior into a bunch of arbitrary categories. We probably all do this to some degree, often subconsciously. We disguise our unhealthy behavior to hide it from ourselves."

Instead of money, let's think about food—specifically, unhealthy desserts. A man trying to lose weight might tell himself, *I haven't had a doughnut in a long time* and then eat one. No big deal. That slip-up alone won't ruin his weight-loss plan. But maybe the next day, at the store, he stops in the candy aisle. *I haven't had Milk Duds in forever.* At a birthday party that weekend: *Hey, when was the last time I had a piece of cake*? On and on it goes—new excuses every day.

Back to Will Smith. Once the big money started rolling in, it's understandable that he wanted to play with his newfound riches (fun!) more than he wanted to think about whether each purchase was a smart move financially (boring). He might have told himself, *I'm a multimillionaire, so I can afford this sports car.* That was true. Ten million dollars minus a sports car is still many millions of dollars. But he might have also thought, *I'm a multimillionaire, so I can afford these high-end motorcycles, this jewelry, these shopping sprees with all my friends*, and so on. Because no one ever taught him to monitor his Whole Money Picture, Smith turned a lot of purchases—none very risky by themselves for a young man with his bank account—into a spending pattern that slowly led to financial disaster. (Temporarily, at least. Smith went on to become one of Hollywood's wealthiest A-list celebrities.)

## Would You Like Endorphins with That?

Okay, so we like to trick ourselves into behaviors that are fun even though on some level we know they're not good for us. That's one reason so many people seem to go out of their way not to monitor their Whole Money Picture. But let's get to the more basic question: why do we find spending so much fun in the first place?

There are a lot of reasons we feel compelled to spend, and we'll explore a bunch of them in this book. But let's start with one of the simplest. As Dr. Patel explains, we're biologically hardwired to do it. "Spending money releases endorphins, which are chemicals that send signals of relief or happiness to the brain. Their real job is to block signals of pain and stress, which is why the body releases them when we get injured or feel anxious. But they also get released when we do things we enjoy, like playing a sport, eating foods we like, and yes, spending money. That's where we get the term 'retail therapy.'"

A picture is starting to emerge here. Spending money makes us feel good—literally, at a chemical level. But logically, we all know spending too much can get us into money trouble. So our brains devise clever tricks to let us keep producing those retail-therapy endorphins without alerting the rational side of our brain that we're draining our bank accounts.

And those tricks work. A 2021 survey found that 56 percent of Americans didn't know how much money they spent in the previous month.[4] So there's your first tip.

## Track Your Whole Money Picture

We'll talk about budgets in Chapter 14, but the key takeaway here is that you'll need one to effectively track your Whole Money Picture. Your budget doesn't need to be fancy or complicated. Just write down how much money you have, how much you're bringing in, and how much you're spending. You can use a spreadsheet, a budgeting app, or even paper and pen. Often just seeing your purchases written down or seeing how much money you're blowing on a specific category of stuff—say, clothing or entertainment—can jolt you into realizing you're overspending. *Hmm.* Maybe that's why more than half the population prefers not to look. They choose the endorphins over financial security.

If young Will Smith had kept a budget as he began spending his $10 million, he would've had plenty of warning that things were moving in the wrong direction financially. And the chances are high that this smart, mathematically savvy guy would've reined in his spending long before he heard the IRS knocking on his door.

## Life Hack: Go to the Gym, Not the ATM

Now you have a scientific strategy to avoid unhealthy spending habits. If spending releases the same feel-good hormones we get from things like exercise—and if we spend money at least in part to release those hormones—then why not just exercise instead of buying stuff? That strategy is healthier *and* cheaper. If you want to let loose some natural, feel-good chemicals, engage in an activity you enjoy. Go for a swim or a hike, head to the gym, or grab a snack (a healthy one). Always keep this in mind: spending is not a sport. And despite the saying, it's not therapy either.

By the way, we're going to review a lot of life hacks like this in the coming chapters. But I want to make clear upfront that the goal of this book isn't to convince you that spending money is bad. Quite the opposite. I want you to be able to use money to enjoy your life. That's what it's for. But for that to happen, you'll need to develop a healthy relationship with money—something many people never do.

My goal is to help you understand many of the subtle, sometimes-hidden causes behind poor money-management decisions. If we can take these psychological, emotional, and even biological explanations out of their hiding places and give you a good look at them, you'll be better prepared to recognize them when they show up. That can take away some of the power they might otherwise have over you—and protect you from making a lot of really stupid money decisions you'll regret.

> **KEY TAKEAWAYS**
>
> - Tracking and understanding your Whole Money Picture is essential to helping you make smart money decisions.
> - Before any purchase, ask yourself if the thing is going to give you real value or if something else—like boredom or stress—might be driving you to buy it.
> - Remember: spending money is neither a sport nor therapy.

When you make money decisions without considering how they'll affect your Whole Money Picture, what you're really doing is putting a future version of yourself in financial jeopardy. So in the next chapter, we'll talk about how you can protect *that* person: Monday Me.

# 2

# *Protect Monday Me*

Morgan is saving up to go on a trip with friends in a couple of months. Birthday money, cash from odd jobs—whenever she brings in a few bucks, she puts that money right into her trip fund. So far, so good.

Then one day Morgan goes to the mall, wanders into the Apple Store, and spots a new headset. She already has a headset, and it works fine. But it's a bit outdated, and she's bored with it. This one looks so sleek that she can't resist. She plunks down every dollar she's saved and buys it.

Fast-forward two months. That trip is now a few days away, and Morgan doesn't have enough money to cover her share. She's going to miss a vacation she's been excited about for months. All for a headset that isn't so new or exciting anymore. In a few days, Morgan will be sitting in her room, looking at her two headsets, watching her friends' adventures unfold on social media.

One way to avoid painful missteps like this is to start looking out for Monday Me. This is the idea that if you spend frivolously today, you're borrowing (better term: stealing) from a future you. If you buy something on Friday out of boredom, what happens on Monday when you need that money for something important? Friday Me will have cheated Monday Me.

## It's Not Just for Mondays

You can use this strategy for any money decision, big and small. Wondering if you should buy that outfit? Think of Next Week Me, or even Tomorrow Me. Then ask yourself, *Will Tomorrow Me have a better use for this cash? Will Next Week Me?* If you have the chance to earn some money but you're not sure if you want to take on the work, consider Next Month Me or Summertime Me. That person will probably be glad you took on the job and banked a few bucks.

Am I suggesting you should always choose to save, work more hours, or be on the lookout for new money-earning opportunities? Not at all. You know your Whole Money Picture better than anyone else. When you've thought through your financial situation—including what's best for your future self—you might decide the right thing is to buy the item or to turn down the job. In those situations, your instinct is probably right. Monday Me will understand. The point is, whenever you make any financial decision, you'll want to keep Monday Me in mind.

This strategy might sound obvious, but a huge percentage of adults treat their money like they rarely give a thought to Monday Me. A 2024 study found nearly half of all credit card users carry debt with them month after month.[1] In fact, at the end of 2024, the average US cardholder with an unpaid balance owed more than $7,000.[2] Millions of people let shortsighted spending impulses dig them into a deeper and deeper financial hole. They might be having fun in the moment, but their Monday Me always gets stuck paying the bill.

Jerry Markell, a Certified Public Accountant based in Southern California, told me he's seen many clients suffer the awful consequences of reckless spending by their younger selves. Here's what he's concluded: "No mindless purchase today will ever be as satisfying as feeling rich tomorrow."

## Facing the Facts

Why do so many people create such big financial problems for their future selves? We can find one reason in science. A clever study at UCLA found that after young people saw an artificially aged image of their faces (generated with AI aging software), they expressed a greater intention to save for retirement. One of the study's co-authors, Hal Hershfield, PhD, offered this key explanation: "We tend to think about our future selves as if they are someone else, wholly different from who we are today."[3]

Interesting, isn't it? If you can see yourself in the future—in this case, literally, by looking at a virtual photo of an older you—you're more likely to identify with and try to help that person. That will make it easier to do things that feel difficult today, like saving your money, eating well, studying hard, or putting in the work on some challenging project. You'll understand that on the other side of those accomplishments, it'll be you who reaps the benefits.

But the reverse is also true. If you can't feel any real connection to your future self, if that person seems like someone else, it becomes much easier to focus on satisfying your wants today even if you know doing so will hurt a future version of you.

Unfortunately, it seems to be human nature to think of our future selves as other people. Dr. Hershfield also said, "A brain-imaging study I coauthored found the brain activity patterns that are evoked by thoughts about a *future self* are quite similar to the brain activity that arises when we think about *other people today*."[4]

This might explain why 88 percent of people give up on their New Year's resolutions within two weeks.[5] Every New Year's Eve, we make these challenging promises—lose weight, improve our grades, get organized—thinking some *other* person will live up to those promises. But if it's New Year's Eve and you hate exercising, then your future self in early January probably won't feel like doing it, either.

Which brings us to how you can benefit from the Monday Me concept. One key to consistently making smarter decisions with your money, decisions that will support and enrich you in the future, is to think about that future person as you. But because our brains naturally have trouble doing so, we need to find you a way around this challenge. One solution is to use the right language, phrases that reinforce the fact that you in four weeks will still be you. So start calling that person Next Month Me.

---

**Get into the Monday Me habit. Make it fun. Say things like, "I'm saving this for Saturday Me," and "Thanks, Last Week Me, for leaving me this cash."**

---

Comedian Gilbert Gottfried has a great line: "Back in the 1400s, people used to walk around going, 'This is a long time ago.'"[6] That joke works because we recognize how ridiculous it is that anybody would ever say *This is a long time ago*. It's never a long time ago, just like it's never a long time from now. We live every minute now. In the 1400s, the 1400s were *now*.

Remembering this joke is another way to reinforce the importance of protecting Monday Me. Next year, it will be now, just as it's now today. And Next Year Me will definitely be grateful if you've made all your money decisions with that person's well-being in mind.

## Life Hack: Treat Saving as a Gift to Future You

Speaking of making Next Year Me grateful, you might also find it helpful to view saving money as giving yourself a gift down the road. I know it's difficult to imagine that next year will ever get here. But it will. (Just ask Last Year Me!) You'll still be you, with all the wants and needs you have right now. Probably some new ones, too. Think about how happy you'll be that Last Year Me left you this gift. When you save money, in fact, it's as if a future you will be getting an inheritance—and nobody has to die.

Treating your spending decisions this way can actually make it fun not to spend money because you can think about how excited the future you—Next Week Me, Next Month Me, Next *Decade* Me—will be to see all the cash you've left.

## Life Hack: Use the Age-Imaging App

Let's go back to that UCLA study. The researchers found that looking at an AI-generated picture of their older selves got people thinking more seriously about saving for their future. So why not try that yourself? Download a free age-progression app and give your future self a look whenever you're considering a big money decision.

You don't need to age your face twenty or thirty years, as the study's participants did. If you're thinking about spending money you know you'd benefit from having in the next couple of years—for college or a car—ask the app to make you look like Two Years from Now Me. Can you look that person in the eyes and say, *I'm spending our college-fund money today*?

Will this have any effect on your financial decisions? Who knows? But it couldn't hurt to try. It might even be fun to meet your older self.

> **KEY TAKEAWAYS**
> - Make saving easier by reminding yourself that the recipient will be *you*.
> - Get in the habit of using Monday Me language. Start saying things like, "If I buy this now, will it hurt Next Week Me?"
> - Before making any big purchases, use an AI face-aging app to look your older self in the eye.

Like getting better at monitoring your Whole Money Picture, developing the habit of protecting Monday Me will take practice. It won't be easy, either, especially if you're not used to having a plan for your money. But not having that plan can lead to other big problems as well. So next, we'll examine what happens when people get caught in a Spending Rip Current.

# 3

# *Avoid the Spending Rip Current*

Steve Martin has a great line about how ridiculous our spending habits can become as our earnings go up. "I bought some pretty good stuff. Got me a $300 pair of socks. Got a fur sink. An electric dog polisher. A gasoline-powered turtleneck sweater. And of course, I bought some dumb stuff, too."[1] Those purchases sound so insane that you know he's joking. But what if I gave you a different quote and told you Nicolas Cage said it? *I bought a nine-foot-tall burial tomb, a set of shrunken pygmy heads, a $150,000 pet octopus, and a $276,000 dinosaur skull.* Obviously, another joke, right? Nope. I made up the quote, yes, but the details in it are all true.[2]

The way Nicolas Cage famously burned through his estimated $150 million fortune, you could get the impression he was trying to go broke. He also bought fifteen multimillion-dollar homes, a deserted island in the Bahamas, and a two-headed snake, which set him back about $80,000.[3] Even Steve Martin couldn't have made that one up.

We can't know for sure what motivated any of his money decisions. But it's clear Cage got caught in what we can think of as a Spending Rip Current. To understand what that means, and how it can cause you so much money trouble, check out the mayhem unleashed by actual rip currents.

## Let's Go to the Beach

Every year in the United States, tens of thousands of beachgoers need to be rescued by lifeguards after getting caught in a *rip current*. This dangerous phenomenon is a narrow channel of water in the ocean rushing quickly and forcefully away from shore. Imagine someone standing on the beach holding a giant fire hose that's blasting water into the ocean at 8 feet per second. If you're caught in a rip current, instinct will tell you to swim as hard as you can straight for shore. But you'll never make it. As the National Ocean Service says, "Rip currents can move faster than an Olympic swimmer." These nature-made monsters are so powerful, in fact, that they kill an estimated 100 people every year.[4]

There is a safe way out of these things, which I'll explain below. But for now, back to the Spending Rip Current.

---

**Like the simple strategy to save yourself from a rip current in the ocean, you can avoid the Spending Rip Current by changing your spending habits just a little.**

---

## Why the Pull to Spend?

Just like a rip current in the ocean, a Spending Rip Current is a set of powerful forces pulling on you financially, causing you to spend and spend. Often you won't even know why.

How do they happen? Why do so many of us get caught in this terrible pattern that can evaporate our bank accounts and even wipe out a movie star's $150 million fortune? As I said above, the Spending Rip Current comes from a *set* of forces, so let's look at a few of the big ones.

### 1. Emotional triggers

You might remember Dr. Patel explaining in Chapter 1 that shopping can release endorphins, and that these feel-good hormones are actually there to protect us from pain and stress. That might give us another clue about what's going on here.

A large body of research has shown that people spend money as a coping mechanism for emotional challenges they're facing. A 2023 study found that 27 percent of all Americans spend to deal with stress. The numbers are higher for Gen Z (35 percent) and higher still for Millennials (43 percent).[5] The phenomenon is so prevalent, in fact, that the report points out there's even a name for it now: "doom spending."

This makes intuitive sense. If someone gets caught in a bad place emotionally, a fun new purchase might give them temporary relief—a short-lived rush of endorphins or their close cousin, the feel-good neurotransmitter dopamine.

But if that behavior becomes a *habit*, both problems only get worse. Owing money triggers stress and feelings of depression. The person tries to cope with those emotions by spending more money. And that kickstarts a cycle leading to both more stress and more debt.

### 2. Habit formation

Speaking of habits, our brains are habit-forming machines, and for good reason. Developing habits played an important role in human evolution and survival. When our cave-dwelling ancestors wanted to protect themselves at night from bears and lions, they probably got into the habit of going through some sort of safety checklist before bedtime, so they wouldn't forget an important safety measure. *Make sure the fire isn't visible in the distance? Check. Put the spear within arm's reach? Check. Hang the "No Soliciting" sign on the cave door? Check.*

Now those habit-making genes are encoded in your DNA. You probably engage in all sorts of habits every day, many of them without thinking. One study found that 43 percent of people's daily activity is simply habit.[6] We often complete these habit-based actions before our conscious mind even knows what happened. Steven Stosny, PhD, wrote in *Psychology Today* that "Habits are processed in the brain thousands of times faster than intentional behavior."[7]

Think about that. If you develop the habit of shopping online whenever you start to feel bored, anxious, or depressed, you'll be clicking "Buy" before your rational mind has the chance to give that purchase a moment's thought.

### 3. Credit cards

As you can see, those first two forces are connected. Lots of people spend money hoping to drown out negative feelings. Sure enough, thanks to those friendly endorphins, the strategy can work, at least for a short time. If they chase that short-term relief over and over, these people could turn their spending into a *habit*—and now we've got a problem.

But that problem becomes turbocharged when we add a third force contributing to the Spending Rip Current: credit cards. We'll dig into this topic in Chapter 10, but for now just understand that one of the risks of using a credit card is that it removes an important psychological tool designed to protect us from getting into money trouble. Years ago, a study by MIT psychologists found that people treat their money much more carefully when they have to pay cash than when they use a card. As the report summary puts it, credit cards are dangerous because "They disconnect the pleasure of buying with the pain of paying."[8]

In other words, one key guardrail against making a stupid purchase is the hesitation you might feel as you reach into your pocket to hand over a bunch of cash. But that protection disappears when you can just load a credit card number into your Amazon account, hit "Buy Now," and not worry about paying for weeks or months. *Spending Rip Current, here we come.*

## Lifeguard!

Before we get into strategies for avoiding the Spending Rip Current, here are two tips the National Ocean Service advises to survive a real one in the ocean. Although rip currents can stretch as much as a half-mile out to sea, they're usually narrow, only 20 or 30 feet across.

So instead of wasting your energy trying to paddle straight back to land, you can swim just a few strokes to either side, parallel to the shore. Soon, you'll be out of the rip current and able to swim casually to safety. Or, if you're not comfortable doing that you can just float and call for help. A rip current pulls you away from the shore, but it won't pull you under the water.[9]

## Life Hack: Make a New Habit

Now let's talk about how to protect yourself against a Spending Rip Current. In the *Psychology Today* article I mentioned earlier, Dr.

Stosny wrote that because of how powerful habits become, "The only reliable way to change an entrenched habit is to develop a new one that is incompatible with the one you want to change."[10]

There's your first strategy. If you want to undo a spending habit, or prevent one from starting, make a new habit that wouldn't allow you to spend without thinking about it.

For example, give yourself a spending allowance. Maybe you'll spend only 30 percent of whatever money you bring in. Or maybe you'd prefer to wall off your spending by time—so you'll let yourself shop for fun stuff only one day every two weeks. The details don't really matter. The point is, if you're someone who sets a self-imposed limit on spending, you can't also be the type of person who gets pulled along by a Spending Rip Current. Those two habits can't really exist within the same person. So you'll be building a new habit, rewiring your brain with a more positive money-management routine.

Here's another idea for a new habit: Create a short checklist of questions to ask yourself before any purchase:

- Am I buying this because I really want or need it?
- Could I be buying this just because I'm bored or anxious?
- Could I be buying this to keep up with my friends?
- Do I really know why I want this?
- Will I soon be bored with this?
- Am I going to care about this thing in a month, a week, even tomorrow?

Often, stopping to ask yourself even a few of these questions before you buy something will uncover the fact that you're less enthusiastic about the thing than you thought at first. That's because these questions will force your brain to think logically and rationally. Once you get those centers of your brain activated, it'll be harder for the sneakier parts of your brain to trick you into spending just for the endorphins or the fun. Try this just a few times, and you'll be on your way to creating a *healthy new habit*—one that Protects Monday Me.

## Life Hack: Swim Sideways Just a Little

Just as you can escape an ocean rip current by swimming parallel for just a few strokes until you're out of its narrow channel, you can adjust your spending habits even a little to stay out of a Spending Rip Current.

Instead of visiting social media platforms or eCommerce stores every time you find a free few minutes, set some modest limits on how often you check those sites. If you like to go to the mall with friends every week, try pulling back to once every few weeks. Also, give some thought to the times of day or days of the week when you tend to spend money. If you can get into the habit during those times of avoiding situations where you might feel tempted to buy stuff, that could help, too.

You don't need big changes to your money routines for this to work. I'm suggesting that you move sideways only a bit. You can still visit all the same social sites and physical stores you like; just do it less frequently. The point is to make your spending decisions more intentional, so that your autopilot habit brain can't sneak silly purchases past you. Just think of it as swimming sideways a little on your personal-finance journey.

> **KEY TAKEAWAYS**
>
> - A Spending Rip Current can result from a habit you're not even aware you've created.
> - People often spend not because they really want something but to alleviate stress or sadness.
> - The best way to avoid a Spending Rip Current, or any entrenched habit, is to replace it with a healthier habit—like setting a spending limit for yourself.

No matter how many things you buy in a Spending Rip Current, they won't make you happier for long. That's one problem. But there's another. As the short-term excitement of these purchases wears off, you'll be piling up a bunch of stuff you don't want. So let's talk next about Tomorrow's Junk.

# 4

# *Don't Buy Tomorrow's Junk*

Imagine you just got something you've really wanted—let's say a new pair of shoes. You take them out of the box, set them on your desk, and stare at them. You can't believe they're yours. Great feeling, isn't it? Maybe you have trouble falling asleep at first because you keep turning on the nightlight for one more look. In fact, the shoes are the only things you notice in your room. Everything else is just background clutter.

Now it's a week later. You've worn the shoes every day, and you still like them. But your excitement? Gone. You hardly think about them anymore. Why would you? They're only shoes.

Wait—what just happened? How can the same items that wowed you last week, even kept you up that first night, hardly catch your eye now? Biologists would say you're experiencing *habituation*. That's a fancy way of saying the more we get used to something, the less it affects us. Ever walk into a restaurant and notice how loud the place is, but then realize a few minutes later that you've completely tuned out the noise? That's habituation at work.

And did you notice the word starts with *habit*? Another way to understand what happened here is that you developed a habit of owning this pair of shoes. As we discussed earlier, your conscious mind doesn't pay much attention to habits. That's why, after only a week, you've already tuned out your new shoes. I describe this as buying Tomorrow's Junk.

## A Path to Nowhere

The classic example of Tomorrow's Junk is the treadmill. Millions of people have had a similar experience with this expensive fitness product. They see an ad or video showcasing its life-changing benefits, and they order one. Then the sad journey of the treadmill begins.

### The Six Life Phases of the In-Home Treadmill

- Phase 1: Exciting new possession promising a healthier life for its owners.
- Phase 2: Ignored by everyone in the home.
- Phase 3: Source of increasing shame and excuses. (*I think barbells are better than treadmills for fitness.*)
- Phase 4: Clothes hanger. (*Hey, can you grab my jacket? It's on the treadmill.*)
- Phase 5: Taken out to the garage. (*At least I got some exercise moving it. Ha ha.*)
- Phase 6: Listed on Facebook Marketplace.

Lots of things can prompt us to buy Tomorrow's Junk. Sometimes by making a purchase, we get to envision the new item making us happier and better off. People buy fancy journals imagining they'll become writers, and treadmills imagining they'll start rigorous workout routines. These purchases can let us enjoy a wonderful picture of our near-term future selves—without doing any of the work to turn that vision into reality. If you've had the experience of getting excited about a new purchase but then finding that excitement is completely gone the moment the item arrives, you've experienced Tomorrow's Junk.

There's also another reason you might fall into this trap. As you learned in the previous chapter, your brain is an excellent habit-creator. Turns out, it's also highly skilled at the opposite of forming habits: looking for new things. This might explain why you (or at least some part of your brain) felt so excited about buying those shoes.

---

Many of the things you want today—even things you really, really want—will soon become Tomorrow's Junk.

---

## Anybody Want to Buy a Dinosaur Skull?

What compels people to buy things they don't need and might not even want? There are many reasons, and they're often hidden from the buyers themselves. Maybe they want to keep up with their friends, or show off to their friends, or just feel like they're the type of person who can afford to buy the thing (even if they can't). We'll explore those motivations in the book's final part: Navigating the Social Side of Money. For now, though, let's talk about our drive to experience novelty.

According to a neurobiology study from the University of Massachusetts Medical School, "The brain is hardwired to seek out stimuli that are new."[1] Identifying new things, beneficial or harmful, would have clearly played a key role in the earliest humans' survival. And because evolution is such a slow process, modern humans still get a quick hit from our brains' reward centers when we expose ourselves to something new.

So we probably buy some things simply because our million-year-old brains crave the novelty reward. That's okay if whatever we're buying gives us real value aside from the short-term rush of dopamine or endorphins. But if it won't, if that need for a quick reward is really the only thing driving our purchase, then we might be buying Tomorrow's Junk. You can't get much more novel than Nicolas Cage's famous purchases, and he no doubt felt great buying those things at first. But one day, he probably found himself standing in his living room wondering, *What am I supposed to do with a dinosaur skull?*

## Can You Believe "Declutter" Is a Real Word?

To get a sense of just how much of the stuff we buy becomes Tomorrow's Junk, let's look at the recent trend of decluttering. Long story short: the average American home today has 300,000 items.[2] Understandably, people are starting to feel that their stuff is invading their personal space. That's leading to a growing industry of consultants to help people clear away their Tomorrow's Junk. The National Association of Productivity and Organizing Professionals (yep, that's a real thing) has more than 3,500 members—all professional declutters.[3]

On the several-hundred-thousand-year scale of human evolution, this concept is five seconds old. People in the 1700s (*Hey, this is a long time ago!*) never felt the need to declutter. Why would they? They didn't have the free time, the wealth, the mass-production technologies, or the Amazon Prime to worry about acquiring too much stuff in the first place. And if our *recent* ancestors didn't have this clutter problem, it's even sillier to imagine it ever crossed the minds of prehistoric humans. But let's have some fun trying.

**Scene: The Prehistoric Cave of Married Couple Steve and Margaret**

> Steve: *Margaret, you've got to stop bringing home all these decorative rocks. They're piled up all over the cave. We're running out of space.*
> 
> Margaret: *Only if you stop collecting all those stupid knives. Same thing.*
> 
> Steve: *That's ridiculous. A knife is a survival tool.*
> 
> Margaret: *Steve, you've got two hands. We have like a hundred knives in this cave. Explain how knife number sixty-three is necessary for our survival.*
> 
> Steve: *Everywhere I look—rocks, rocks, rocks! I can't even see what I'm doing.*
> 
> Margaret: *And I keep stubbing my toes on the knives you leave all over the floor. I'm going to trip over one of those things and die. They're really the opposite of survival tools.*
> 
> Steve: *I guess you're right, Margaret. We both need to stop acquiring so much unnecessary stuff. Think we can afford to hire a decluttering professional?*
> 
> Margaret: *Only if we can pay him in knives.*

Our ancient ancestors had far more serious concerns than overconsumption or a cluttered cave: predatory animals, disease, starvation, and freezing to death in winter. They had to devote most of their time and energy to surviving the day. We're incredibly lucky to be living in modern times instead of back then. But the Tomorrow's Junk problem has health dangers of its own.

A study by UCLA researchers found that when people live in cluttered environments, their bodies produce more of the stress hormone cortisol.[4] Prolonged elevated cortisol levels have been linked to serious health problems including bone loss, blood clots, depression, and even heart attacks.[5]

So we're back to another vicious cycle, like the one we encountered in the previous chapter, where debt makes us feel stressed, which leads us to spend money, but the spending only puts us deeper in debt, creating more stress.

In this case, the dangerous cycle looks like this: chasing the exciting feeling of novelty leads us to buy more and more things, which leads to clutter, which spikes our stress, which sends us back to buying more and more things. *Hello, Tomorrow's Junk.*

The decluttering movement is actually a hopeful sign. It means people are starting to realize that overconsumption can lead to real problems in their lives. I do find it disappointing that what's slowing down these people's out-of-control spending isn't concern for their financial well-being but rather the fact that it's making their homes less livable. Whatever their reasons, though, if it means people are buying less of Tomorrow's Junk, the decluttering movement is a positive trend for society.

But let's talk about you. What can you do to avoid falling into the Tomorrow's Junk trap in the first place?

## Life Hack: Leave It in the Cart

Now that you're familiar with the Monday Me concept, you have one tool to avoid Tomorrow's Junk that most people don't. If you're considering a purchase, first, slow things down. Step back from your computer or phone and give yourself a minute to think. That'll help you prevent your endorphin-seeking habit-brain from taking over and clicking the Buy button too quickly.

Your next step is to bring Monday Me into the discussion. Ask yourself, *How about it, Next Month Me* (or Next Week Me or even Tomorrow Me): *Are we happy I made this purchase? Still enjoying the thing? Or did I stick you with Tomorrow's Junk?*

You might also want to make Right Now Me wait a bit longer. Tell yourself you'll come back to the item in a day. If you still see value in the purchase, you can go for it. But guess what? In many cases, you won't. Something else was driving your desire for that purchase—novelty, boredom, anxiety, a craving for endorphins—and not the product itself. My wife has a clever strategy in these situations. She'll put an item in an online shopping cart and leave the site. In most cases, she doesn't even remember she did it. And if she returns to the site later, she often has no idea why she saved the item to her cart.

## Life Hack: Make Tomorrow Me Earn It

Another strategy is to give yourself a small test or obstacle to make sure you really want the item. In the case of the treadmill, before making that purchase, you could spend a few days going for runs or walks. If you meet that commitment, then you have a better sense that you'll actually use the treadmill when it arrives. (Better idea, though: just keep going for the runs or walks. Exercise plus fresh air beats exercise alone. Although you will need to find another place to hang your jacket.)

> **KEY TAKEAWAYS**
>
> - Before you buy something, stop and imagine a few days or weeks in the future. Still thrilled you bought it? If not, it might be Tomorrow's Junk.
> - Be careful: Your brain is hardwired to seek novelty and can trick you into thinking you want some new thing when it just wants a quick rush.
> - If you're not sure if an item you're thinking about buying is Tomorrow's Junk, ask Tomorrow Me.

So far, we've been discussing only internal causes of poor money decisions, how our own psychology and biology can lead us into financial missteps. Those are important things to know. But to become a true money-savvy powerhouse, you also need to be aware of the many external influences out there trying to separate you from your money. So in the next chapter, we'll discuss one of the biggest challenges in this category: the advertising industry. Let me help you Dodge the Ad Barrage.

# 5

# *Dodge the Ad Barrage*

We've been shining a light on hidden biological and psychological triggers that cause people to spend money for the wrong reasons: chasing novelty, a rush of feel-good hormones, or just to fight off boredom. One reason people find so many of their purchases unfulfilling is that it's often these unconscious triggers, not rational decisions about the products, that drive their spending decisions. But do you know who's fully aware that these unconscious motivations are steering us to plunk down our money? Advertisers. In fact, they spend billions of dollars a year trying to *activate* these emotional triggers in our brains.

They're not even hiding it. Here's a quote from legendary advertising executive Leo Burnett: "Good advertising does not just circulate information. It penetrates the public mind with desires and beliefs."[1] Yikes.

Think about what Burnett is saying. The goal of the advertising industry is to sneak into your brain, tiptoe around your rational thoughts, and implant feelings and ideas that will serve the advertisers' goals. Then they can persuade you to buy stuff you don't need, don't want, and don't even know why you're buying. Burnett was so successful at this totally creepy strategy that *TIME Magazine* named him one of the "100 most influential people of the twentieth century."[2] Double yikes.

## Winners Buy Our Stuff

It's unfair to pick on Burnett. He's just doing his job. Every year, businesses release millions of new products they need to sell. Competition for your spending dollar is fierce. Also, most consumer products today are high quality. That's great news for us because it means the things we buy tend to last a long time. But consider what it means for a company like Nike. If their shoes last for many years, how will they convince you to buy more of them before your current pair wears out?

If Nike didn't have advertising, their conversation with a customer might look like this.

> Nike: *Hey, would you like to buy a new pair of basketball shoes?*
> Customer: *I already own a pair of Nikes, and they're holding up well. Thanks for making such great shoes.*
> Nike: *Oh. Well, thanks. Glad to hear it. Come see us when they start falling apart.*
>
> Obviously, that won't cut it for Nike. They want to sell you more than one pair of shoes. So they hire an advertising agency, and that agency exploits all the unconscious motivations in your mind that we've been talking about. So now the conversation sounds a bit different.
>
> Nike Advertisers: *Hey, would you like to buy a new pair of basketball shoes?*
> Customer: *I already own a pair of Nikes, and they're still holding up. Thanks for making such great shoes.*

Nike Advertisers: *Those old things? Ha! We've released new ones, and your friends are already wearing them. You don't want your friends to laugh at you, right?*

Customer: *I hadn't even thought about that. Do you think my friends will be impressed if I show up wearing the new Nikes?*

Nike Advertisers: *Well, they won't be laughing at you. And did you see the game the other night? The high scorer was wearing Nikes. You want to be a better player, don't you?*

Customer: *Of course. But as I said, I already have a pair of—*

Nike Advertisers: *The player was wearing the* new *Nikes. Not the old ones you're still clinging to. Keep up.*

*Keep up.* That's actually a good summary of most advertising messages. Many of them are designed to create feelings of lack, anxiety, and maybe even shame. In other words, to create problems you can solve only by keeping up—buying whatever the advertiser is selling. And you might be surprised at just how frequently advertisers are hitting you with these messages. According to researchers at the University of Southern California, we see about 5,000 ads every day.[3]

Billboard ads, web ads, commercials on TV and radio, mobile ads, paid search ads, social ads, and on it goes. And those are just the ones that are upfront about their ad-ness. A lot of your entertainment content sneaks in disguised advertisements as well. Here are a few examples:

- **Product placement in movies, music, TV, and games**

When a movie character pulls out a Microsoft laptop, drinks a can of Coke, or hops into a Dodge Durango, those are often a form of paid advertising called *product placement*. The brand gets its product woven into a piece of entertainment you're enjoying, and the movie or TV producers earn another source of money from the production.

- **Entertainers on talk shows discussing their new projects**

When an actor has a new movie out or a musician is about to release a new album, they'll often appear as guests on TV talk shows, radio shows, and popular podcasts to promote their new product. Viewers are happy to see these celebrities chatting with the hosts, but these celebs are often there only because their movie or record contract demands that they make promotional appearances like these. The fact that these shows or YouTube videos break away for paid commercials only confuses the issue. Just understand that when they come back to the show itself—to continue the celebrity interview—you're still watching an ad message.

- **Celebrities wearing designers' clothing at public appearances**

Advertisers see famous people as walking, talking billboards for their clients' products. When you see a celebrity wearing a dress, hat, handbag, watch, or other accessories at an awards show or movie premiere, there's a good chance the brand is actually paying them to wear their products. They're counting on you wanting to be like that celeb—and thinking that buying the same products will help.

- **Influencers talking about products on social media**

Brands and their ad agencies pay influencers a fortune to review and talk up their products in videos, podcasts, and other social content. They're borrowing the credibility these influencers have earned, hoping their followers will believe that if the influencer likes the products, they should too. Most of these personalities are upfront about their business relationships and will acknowledge when and by whom they're getting paid. But there's a gray area. Sometimes in their posts, they'll talk up a product sponsoring their channel but not mention that fact. Just be aware that although this content looks organic, there's often a brand paying your favorite influencer to persuade you.

---

**Ask yourself before a purchase,** *Am I buying this because I decided I want it? Or because an advertiser decided for me?*
**That's how you'll Dodge the Ad Barrage.**

---

You're bombarded every day with messages produced by people like Leo Burnett—people who want to sneak into your mind, uninvited, and plant new "desires and beliefs" in there to benefit the brands paying them.

It might help to understand how advertising agencies achieve these goals. One strategy is to employ smart people with titles like Consumer Psychologist, Market Research Scientist, and Consumer Behavior Analyst. Their job is to study you, to learn your hopes and fears, so they know which emotional buttons to push. These advertising scientists (creepy concept, isn't it?) then group you into *psychographics*: categories of people with a common set of attitudes, opinions, and lifestyles. Let's look at two typical psychographics and how advertisers exploit them both.

1. **The Early Adopter**

Advertisers see you as the cool kid, the trendsetter. You'll take chances. For example, you'll wear something no one else is wearing, ride a bike or a skateboard no one else has, listen to music that's not on popular radio, or even carry an energy drink around school that's different from what the other students are drinking.

So advertisers will try to make you feel like you're a rebel. They'll tell you that you're cool because you don't follow trends—and then they'll try to convince you that whatever they're selling is the choice of rebels like you. They assume that eventually your friends will follow your lead. That's why Consumer Psychologists call them Followers.

**2. The Follower**

Advertisers see you as the type of person who buys out of fear—fear that you won't be cool or liked or welcomed into the group if you don't buy what the advertisers are selling. Harriet Boxer, PhD, a clinical psychologist in California, explained to me that "How someone dresses, such as what brands of shoes or clothing they wear, can signal someone's status or affiliation with a group."

If they view you as a follower, someone who worries about their peers staring or laughing at them, advertisers will try to convince you that whatever they're selling is the safe choice, the thing all your friends are already buying. You'll need to buy this thing too, they'll say, because it's the best way to keep from sticking out and having people point at you.

## And Now, a Sneaky Mind Virus from Our Sponsor

You might be thinking, *Advertisements don't affect me.* Maybe. But keep in mind that this industry pays for most of TV, music, social media, and other forms of entertainment. Businesses in the United States spend more than $400 billion a year on advertising.[4] Would they keep doing that if their ads didn't make us spend?

Look at it this way. Advertisers hit you with 5,000 ads a day. You might tune out almost all of them. But if even 1 percent of those ads successfully "penetrate" your mind "with desires and beliefs" that weren't really yours to begin with, that means you're at least somewhat influenced by fifty ad messages every day. So what can you do?

## Life Hack: Reason Through Your Purchases

Let's say you're a guy and you see an ad on Instagram for an expensive shirt. The ad shows the shirt on the torso of a muscular model (or maybe it's an AI-generated image of a model). You can sense those irrational signals hitting your brain: *Wearing this outfit will make me look like that shredded guy.*

Now ask yourself—and this is the key: do it out loud—*What types of things could I actually do to get more jacked, to look more like that model? Strength training? Sprinting? Jumping rope?* Good answers. Okay, now ask yourself—out loud again—*How about buying a new shirt? Would that help me improve my physique?* Poof! By reasoning through your thoughts out loud, you've just blocked a sneaky advertising trick that gets us all from time to time.

I'm not saying you shouldn't buy the shirt. It might be perfect for you. Subject it to logic: ask Monday Me if you can spare the money. Check in with your Whole Money Picture. Then make a rational decision. But with that simple exercise, you've chased away an advertiser's implanted belief, and you've crossed off one illogical reason to buy the shirt.

## Life Hack: Eavesdrop on Advertisers' Private Chats

The bad news is that advertisers have gotten extremely skilled at manipulating our thoughts and behaviors. The good news, though, is that they're happy to share their best strategies with anyone who will listen. So grab an advertising book like *Positioning: The Battle for Your Mind*. You'll basically be eavesdropping on some of the most successful ad executives as they teach other advertisers how to sneak into your mind to plant new desires and beliefs.

Hearing these advertising geniuses describe their best tactics can take away some of their power over you when you encounter those tactics in an ad message. If this sounds like a boring homework assignment, keep in mind that these are advertisers—in other words, people who know how to make their writing fun to read.

> **KEY TAKEAWAYS**
>
> - Advertisers exist to sneak desires and beliefs into your brain—not to help you find products that are good for you.
> - Before any purchase, talk through your reasoning out loud. That can often expose the clever advertisements' ideas that are truly driving you.
> - To learn how advertisers try to manipulate you, let them tell you directly. Pick up an easy-to-read book like *Positioning*, by Jack Trout and Al Ries.

You're building an impressive set of tools to create smart spending habits. And now you also know to watch out for the sophisticated advertising industry's constant attempts to sneak new needs and wants into your mind. Next, we'll pull all these concepts together and level up your money-management game another notch—by teaching you to Take an Aerial View of your financial life.

# 6

# *Take an Aerial View of Your Finances*

If it's occurred to you that several of the principles we've discussed so far seem similar, you're right. They all share one important theme, which we'll discuss below. First, though, let's do a quick recap.

**1. Know Your Whole Money Picture**

Get familiar with your overall financial situation: how much you have, where it's coming from, how much you're spending, and where it's going. Seeing the whole picture is the only way to know whether you're moving in the right or wrong direction financially. It's also the only way to know if any specific money decision is okay or could hurt you.

**2. Protect Monday Me**

Recognize that future versions of yourself—tomorrow, in a month, two years from now—will all still be you. Get in the habit of naming those people (*Monday Me*, for example) and talk with them about your money decisions. Getting to know your future selves can make them feel real, which can help you make money decisions that'll protect their interests as well.

3. **Avoid the Spending Rip Current**

Step back when you're considering an impulse buy. Try to figure out if what's driving you is interest in the product itself or some other factor: spending out of habit, hoping for an endorphin rush, or because an advertiser has manipulated you. Slowing down a purchase, taking yourself out of autopilot mode, is an effective way to catch these hidden drivers that can lead to a Spending Rip Current.

4. **Don't Buy Tomorrow's Junk**

Subject each potential purchase to a simple test. Ask yourself if the item will bring you enough value over time to make it worth buying. If not—if it's an outfit you'll probably wear once, for example—it might be Tomorrow's Junk. Evaluating the useful life of any purchase can protect you from wasting money and piling up stuff you didn't truly want in the first place.

5. **Dodge the Ad Barrage**

Stay on alert for the many advertisements you're exposed to every day: Dodge the Ad Barrage. Make a conscious effort to look for ads' manipulative emotional triggers. Becoming skilled at spotting advertisers' psychological tricks can help you avoid being manipulated by them—and ensure you buy things for the right reasons.

# We've Reached Money-Savvy Altitude

Did you notice the common theme? Every principle here forces you out of the moment when you're about to make a money decision. It's like freeing you from a hypnotic spell and giving you more context as you evaluate a potential purchase. In other words, these principles are all designed to help you Take an Aerial View of your financial moves.

An Aerial View is the wide field of visibility you have from above—from an airplane, helicopter, or drone camera. Imagine yourself hovering a 100 feet above the ground, looking down and watching yourself living your life. But now imagine that with this wider view, you're able to see not only the current moment, but also the past. From this improved vantage point, you can spot patterns in your behavior over time, patterns you couldn't identify from ground level, where you can see only the present moment.

Let's say that from your Aerial View, you notice that each of the last few times you've gotten your hands on some money, you immediately went out and spent a good portion of it—almost always on stuff that you got bored with quickly (Tomorrow's Junk).

This is great news. You've identified a harmful trend—a Spending Rip Current—that needs correcting. It suggests you've been making financial decisions without considering their effects on even your near-term future self (Monday Me). It's also a clue that you've been spending money for some of the emotional reasons we've reviewed, such as boredom or a misguided idea that some clever advertiser snuck into your mind. These are the bad habits that get adults into serious money trouble, and they help explain one study that found the average American in 2024 was $6,329 in credit card debt.[1] Most of those cardholders will be paying off those debts painfully over many years—and at a final cost of much more than $6,329.

But now that you can Take an Aerial View of your financial behavior over time, you're in a much better position to identify and correct these dangerous habits before they can cause you long-term financial harm.

---

**When you take an Aerial View of your money behavior, you'll find it much easier to spot bad habits—and that's the first step to making better financial decisions.**

## Alexa, TV Volume Down!

If you've read this far, you know there are hidden forces doing everything in their power to prevent you from developing an Aerial View of your money behavior over time. If those forces want you to spend, they don't want you stopping to think through the purchases using context or reason. Here's Dr. Patel again: "If your brain is eager for an endorphin reward and knows that an irrational behavior is the quickest path, it will temporarily block you from accessing its rational regions, so you think only about the reward now, not the consequences you'll have to pay later."

Another way to think about those hidden evolutionary drivers pushing you to buy stuff—like your brain's craving for novelty—is that these forces do their best to scream *Now! Now! Now!* when they want something. That screaming can drown out your logical mind from alerting you that this spending decision isn't actually good for you.

Speaking of drowning out your logical mind, have you ever noticed that the commercials on TV are louder than the shows themselves? TV advertisers have done this for decades. It became such a source of viewer frustration, in fact, that it led to a federal law called the Commercial Advertisement Loudness Mitigation (CALM) Act.[2]

Even though they might technically follow the law today, advertisers still use sound to grab your attention, with sudden loud noises, for example. Those noises, in fact, are designed to hit us on an evolutionary-biology level—forcing us to give them our attention because they might be a threat. *Thanks again, advertisers!*

## That Rip Current Doesn't Look So Scary from up Here

Think back to the rip currents we discussed in Chapter 3. The real ones, in the ocean. You learned that although these dangerous currents can stretch far out to sea, they're usually very narrow, just a few dozen feet wide. That's why the experts recommend that if you're caught in one, you should swim parallel to the shore. After just a few strokes, you'll find yourself out of the rip current's powerful hold.

If you could view the rip current from your Aerial View, hovering over the shoreline in a helicopter, the solution to escaping would be much clearer. You'd see that the rip current is like a long, thin blast of water heading away from shore. It'd be clear to you from above that, while it would be difficult to swim straight against the thing and paddle to land, you could easily move sideways just a few feet and be back in calm ocean water.

Same with taking an aerial view of your spending patterns over time. In the moment, each purchase might have felt logical, even necessary. But as you now examine them all together, from above, you can see that in several of those moments something else was driving you. You were attempting to achieve some emotional or psychological goal by repeatedly buying new things. But just as with a real rip current, you can swim in that direction as hard as possible—make purchase after purchase—and still never reach your goal.

You might also notice that most of the items you bought gave you value only for a short time. And if you look at your Whole Money Picture today, you might realize those previous versions of you cheated Today Me out of cash you should have in your pocket now.

Do you think the typical US adult, who has racked up more than $6,000 in credit card debt, made all those purchases while thinking about Tomorrow's Junk or Taking an Aerial View of their finances? Of course not. And that's why you must. Here are some strategies to help.

## Life Hack: Ask Yourself if the Purchase Fits a Pattern

Now that you have the Aerial View metaphor for identifying patterns, stop and take some time to think through your previous money decisions—maybe over the last three or six months. Go through your eCommerce accounts, receipts, social media posts, or wherever you'll find a record of the things you've bought. (You might want to write this stuff down, so you can see it all in one place and not have to do this exercise from memory.)

Look for patterns in your spending behavior. Have you forgotten about or gotten bored with many of these items? Do you remember how you felt buying them? Did you feel that any of them would make you happier or proud to own them? If so, do any of those items make you feel that way today? Can you remember any purchases where, looking back, you might have been influenced by an ad message or even just a short-term craving for novelty?

Like all the other principles we've discussed, Taking an Aerial View is a great way to drag these hidden emotional drivers out of their hiding places and take a good look at them.

## Life Hack: Enjoy the Accomplishment

As hard as this is to believe, when you get into the habit of Taking an Aerial View of your finances, you might actually find the process fun.

People often talk about saving money, working hard, and other responsible behavior as "delaying gratification." But that's only half right.

Yes, when you make smart decisions about your life, you are setting yourself up to be happier down the road than you'd be if you made reckless or self-destructive decisions. But doing smart things for your future—like developing a healthy relationship with money—will also give you a sense of accomplishment as you're doing them. And that will make you *feel good now.* Try it.

---

**KEY TAKEAWAYS**

- Taking an Aerial View of your financial behavior over time is a great way to identify patterns in your money decisions that need correcting.

- The Aerial View can also help you detect the specific psychological or biological triggers that might steer you to buy for the wrong reasons.

- Developing smarter habits with your money isn't "delaying gratification," because you'll also find the sense of accomplishment gratifying *now*.

---

Okay, you've absorbed a lot of information. You're on your way to becoming an Aerial View-taking, Monday Me-protecting, Ad Barrage-dodging personal finance rockstar. You deserve a break. So in the next chapter, we'll have a little fun—and Gamify Your Money Habits.

# 7

# *Gamify Your Money Habits*

There's an interesting line at the beginning of the gambling movie *Rounders*. "If you can't spot the sucker in your first half-hour at the [poker] table, then you are the sucker."[1] Let's apply a similar philosophy to how we handle our money.

If you're unfamiliar with poker, that's okay. The specifics don't matter here. All you need to know is that this game is primarily not about the cards you're dealt but how well you can read and deceive your opponents. Everyone playing is trying to deceive everyone else. They want to conceal how good (or bad) their cards are, monitor the other players' behaviors to figure out if their cards are good or bad, and manipulate everyone else at the table into making the wrong decisions. That's how we'll think of the game of spending.

Imagine sitting down at a poker table, but instead of playing poker, you're considering a purchase. Your opponents are also seated around the table. One of them (your novelty-seeking brain) wants you to buy the thing because it's chasing the quick reward of something new. So it tries to trick you into imagining how great you'll feel when the thing arrives. Another opponent (an advertiser) tries to plant a worry in your mind that your peers will think less of you if you don't buy the item. Every player around the table has a different deception, bluff, or other trick. If you can't recognize these moves—if you're ready to hit Buy without being able to look around the table and identify the real reason—then you're the sucker.

Let's turn the tables on these deceptive opponents. As we learned in Chapter 3 from Dr. Stosny, the best way to eliminate a negative habit is to replace it with a positive habit that's inconsistent with the one we want to end. A great way to create new habits is to turn them into games. So let's learn some games that put you in control of your financial decisions. Here are a few strategies to Gamify Your Money Habits.

# Ready, Player One?

1. Spot the Advertiser's Hidden Agenda

Every time you see an ad—online, in a video, on an outdoor sign or billboard—try to figure out which emotions the advertiser is trying to trigger. Are they aiming for aspirational (*You can be like this model*) or implanting fear and anxiety (*You don't want your friends to laugh at you*)? Are they playing to your sense of pride (*You're important and awesome*) or your fear of standing out (*Don't be the only one without this*)?

## How to Keep Score

Set challenges for yourself. Try to spot, say, five examples of ads targeted at the Early Adopter psychographic (*You're awesome*) and five others trying to manipulate the Follower (*Don't get left behind*).

You can also set a time limit on your goal—say, five examples of each within one week.

2. The Product Placement Hunt

As you watch movies or TV shows, be on the lookout for those disguised advertisements called *product placements*. Did you notice the logo on a character's handbag? As the star of the movie looked at her watch, did the scene then show you a close-up of her wrist so you could read the watch's brand name? Once you start noticing product placements, you'll see (and hear) them everywhere: social media videos, games, even song lyrics.

## How to Keep Score

Quantify your product placement hunt. See if you can identify two or three examples woven into the entertainment you consume in a day. When you get skilled at spotting these hidden ads, you can increase the challenge by looking for specific types of product placements snuck into entertainment content—like dialogue mentions, wardrobe appearances, prop usages (like a character drinking from a Coke bottle), and brand signage.

---

**Make games out of noticing your spending triggers, spotting advertisers' hidden agendas, and setting goals for saving. These things can be much more rewarding than buying stuff.**

---

3. Days Without Spending

It's so sad that people spend out of boredom. They end up with things they never wanted and missing money they could've enjoyed. With the Days Without Spending game, you can do the opposite: have some fun by *not* spending.

## How to Keep Score

Set specific challenges for yourself. Can you go, say, two weeks without buying anything online or from social media sites? Can you eat only home-cooked meals for a full month, not spending a dollar on food or drinks out?

4. How Much Can You Save?

This game is the flipside of Days Without Spending. You can play both at the same time. Your specific dollar goal isn't as important as the fact that you'll become much more strategic about your purchases. And you'll be piling up money that Monday Me can really enjoy.

## How to Keep Score

For this game to work (and to keep it fun), you'll need both a dollar amount and a timeline. Maybe you'll try to save $200 in the next three months. Whatever challenge you decide on, it needs to be reasonable given your unique circumstances. If you set a goal that's out of reach, or set one that's too easy, you'll get bored and stop playing. Make it an achievable stretch.

5. Meal on a Budget

This one can be lots of fun, especially if you make it a social activity. Set a maximum dollar amount for a lunch or dinner out and try to find a place where you can keep the whole bill (including the tip) under that limit. Invite friends—they'll probably find the challenge fun, too. It involves two things everybody loves: games and eating.

## How to Keep Score

Start with reasonable budget limits. Find funky restaurants, food carts, or other fun places to grab a meal inexpensively—but don't make it so difficult that you won't stick with it. Just rack up small wins at first. As you get more experienced, keep upping your game by lowering your meal budget.

## Retailers Can't Sell You Accomplishment

If we stick with the game metaphor, we can uncover another reason that spending on frivolous stuff rarely solves anyone's problems. Imagine you were playing a board game, and someone picked up your piece and moved it to the finish line. *Congratulations! You win!* Doesn't sound like much fun, does it? Your goal isn't simply to put your piece on the winner's spot; it's to win the game for real. You can't achieve that goal without playing and putting in the effort.

Retailers and advertisers will always promise you a shortcut to feeling like a winner if you purchase their stuff. Unfortunately, you can't buy your way to a sense of accomplishment.

But the good news is that you can *play* your way to a sense of accomplishment—and that includes Gamifying Your Money Habits. Rita Hyman, PhD, a retired clinical psychologist (and my mom!), puts it this way: "Working toward a money-saving goal can be enormously rewarding, and not just when we reach our goal amount, but all along the way. Making progress on a difficult goal gives us a feeling of earned pride and empowerment that we don't find many other places in our lives. Even if it weren't for the financial benefits, I'd still recommend people make a goal of saving money."

Thanks, Mom. Great advice, as usual.

> **KEY TAKEAWAYS**
> - Gamifying Your Money Habits gives you more control over your financial life—and it's fun.
> - Playing these games can boost your skills at identifying hidden drivers that push you to buy stuff you don't need.
> - Buying from retailers can't give you a sense of accomplishment, but succeeding at games like these definitely can.

To this point, we've been talking about spending, saving, and monitoring your money only in the abstract. We haven't discussed the specific tools you'll use to interact with your money day-to-day. So in the next part, we'll review the basics of your Money Toolkit.

*Part II*

# Getting to Know Your Money Toolkit

# 8

# *Checking Accounts*

Fascinating guy, Willie Sutton. The legendary bank robber found ingenious ways to break into buildings, like dropping in through a skylight in the ceiling. He spent years on the FBI's list of Most Wanted Fugitives. And he came up with one of the most famous lines in criminal-justice history. When asked why he robbed banks, Sutton answered, "Because that's where the money is."[1]

Your *checking account* will probably be home base for most of your day-to-day interactions with money. If you want to buy something using a payment app, like Venmo, where will those tiny elves who live inside the Venmo app find your money to pay for it? Probably in your checking account. (I'm not a techie and have no idea how these payment apps work, but I'm pretty sure the process involves elves.) When you swipe your *debit card* to pay for something, where does that money come from? Probably your checking account. (Yes, I know the debit elves don't actually live inside the debit cards. That would be ridiculous. They live inside the machine that reads your card when you swipe it.)

Your checking account is going to play a big role in your financial routine throughout your life. So let's talk about it.

## What Is a Checking Account?

Here's a helpful definition from Bank of America: "A checking account is a type of deposit account that enables customers to deposit funds and withdraw available funds on demand."[2] As Willie Sutton might put it, you'll be using this account for all types of everyday transactions *because that's where your money is.*

Because you'll be depending on your checking account to fund most of your day-to-day spending needs, you'll need to keep it stocked with money. If you have a job, for example, you'll want to direct deposit at least a portion of your paycheck into this account.

The phrase "checking account" is actually outdated. Until the early 2000s, a common method of payment was to write a *check*: a piece of paper that acts as a promise from your bank to pay whatever amount you write on it to whichever person or business you specify. Apartment renters would pay their rent each month by delivering (or mailing) a physical check to their landlord. People would fill out paper checks to pay their energy bills, phone bills, credit card bills, and to make all sorts of other payments.

You can still hear the concept in terms like "paycheck," even though very few businesses still pay their employees with a physical check. The name seems to be sticking for now, but these accounts might soon have a different name. Maybe we'll go back to the more traditional *demand-deposit account*. (They got that name because you could open an account and start withdrawing your money immediately—*on demand*—to pay for various expenses.)

## How a Checking Account Works

Here's how those physical checks worked (and still do, for the few who use them). Imagine you have $3,000 in your checking account, and you need to pay your hair stylist $70 after a cut. If you don't have the cash at the moment, you might take out one of the blank checks your bank gave you, write out your $70 payment, and hand over the check. Your stylist will take the check to their bank, which will ask your bank for the money, and then the $70 will move from your bank account to your stylist's account. As soon as that happens, your checking account balance will drop to $2,930.

Okay, this isn't 1998, so let's replace "write a check" with "Zelle your payment" to your stylist. No paper. No need for your stylist to go to the bank to get the money. But the principle is the same. When you Zelle (or Venmo or Apple Pay) your $70, what's happening is that your bank and your stylist's bank are communicating and agreeing to move the money from one bank to the other.

**Your checking account is home base for your day-to-day financial needs. You'll want to keep enough money in it to pay your expenses—and put any money above that amount into a savings account that pays you interest.**

## You Better Check Yourself

That little scene describes how you should be managing your checking account. But instead of $3,000, let's say you have only $200 in the account when it's time to pay for your haircut. Let's also say that around the same time, you have an automatic payment scheduled for your monthly phone bill. In other words, your phone provider is about to send a payment request to your bank, and the bank is going to pull that money from your checking account to pay it. Your phone bill will be about $150 this month. As you Zelle $70 to your hair stylist, there's a chance the $150 payment has already happened—and you're about to take your account down to negative $20. Unfortunately, millions of people every year make these types of completely avoidable mistakes with their accounts. And as I'll explain below, this screwup is going to cost you. First, though, let's review what's great about having a checking account.

## Cool Things about Checking Accounts

1. **They make payments of all types very convenient**

Checking accounts can make your financial life easier and more convenient. As I noted above, you can link your account to a payment app like Zelle and buy things by simply texting or emailing your payment to the recipient. You can also set regular auto-payments to ensure you always pay your recurring bills on time.

2. **You can deposit money easily**

Thankfully, checking accounts make putting money *into* your account as easy as they make it to take money out. Every checking account with a reputable bank will let you set up direct deposits for regular payments, such as your paycheck from work, sending that money automatically into your account. If you receive a one-off payment through an app like PayPal, you can easily move that money into your checking account with a few keystrokes.

And if you receive a physical check—say, as a birthday gift from a grandparent—you can use your checking account's app to take a picture of the check and deposit the money straight into your account. No visit to a bank is needed.

3. **They make it easy to monitor your spending activity**

Most banks' apps will let you view your checking account history—how much money you've brought in, how much you've spent, what regular payments you're making, and where your money is going. In other words, a banking app tied to your checking account is a great way to keep track of your Whole Money Picture.

## Risks of Misusing a Checking Account

### 1. Overdraft charges

One of the costliest checking account penalties is the *overdraft charge*. This is the fee your bank will charge you if it has to cover a payment you try to make without having enough in your account to pay for it. According to Bankrate.com, the average overdraft fee in 2024 was $27.08. Bankrate's research also found that 94 percent of bank accounts impose these fees.[3]

You can also get hit with an overdraft fee if you're not watching your auto-payments closely. If your account balance gets low enough that you don't have the money to cover your next phone bill—and your bank tries to auto-pay the bill—that could take your account below zero and trigger one of these hefty charges. So you'll need to keep a close watch on all of your money inflows and outflows.

### 2. High costs of ATM mismanagement

Another convenient feature of checking accounts is that they give you an *ATM (automated teller machine) card*, which you can use to withdraw cash from one of the bank's machines. So why didn't I add this to the "cool things" list above? Because it's easy to mishandle an ATM card, and doing so can cost you a lot of cash.

We'll discuss this more in Chapter 12, but the bottom line is that an ATM card is a great tool if you use it *only* at ATMs owned by or affiliated with your bank. Then the service is almost always free. But if you pull out cash from an ATM that's not part of your bank's network, the fees you'll pay are often ridiculously high—an average charge of $4.73 in 2024.[4]

### 3. It can make spending too easy

Back in the Jurassic Period when I opened my first checking account, we had only a few options to pay for things or access our money. We could write a physical check, go to an ATM to withdraw cash from our account, or walk into a bank and ask a teller to give us some of our money. As inconvenient as that was, it did create a natural obstacle to overspending.

The electronic conveniences you'll have with your first checking account—payment apps, a debit card, all those little elves working around the clock—will make it very easy to spend your money. If you're not closely monitoring your checking account activity and keeping an eye on your Whole Money Picture, you could find yourself spending your account down to nothing. Or worse, less than nothing.

## Life Hack: Add Regular Payment Alerts to Your Calendar App

A great way to keep track of regular auto-payments from your checking account is to add them as events on your calendar app. That way, you'll always know exactly when your Netflix or even your credit card payment will get deducted from your account. That's a great way to protect yourself against making purchases when your account is low and you also have auto-payments coming up soon.

## Life Hack: Set Up Low-Balance Alerts

Most checking accounts today can alert you (by text, email, or app notification) if your balance drops below a certain level. Take advantage of this feature, so you'll always have plenty of warning if you're spending too much. It can also help protect you from the dreaded overdraft fee—where a purchase drops you below a zero balance and now you've got to pay a hefty fee to the bank for bailing you out.

Speaking of those overdraft charges, you might want to choose a bank that lets you link your savings and checking accounts to safeguard against spending yourself into negative territory. If you try to make a purchase that takes your checking account below zero, and you have this service, your bank will automatically pull the money from your savings account to cover the purchase. That'll still cost you a small fee, but it will be much less than an overdraft penalty.

## Life Hack: Monitor Your Account Frequently

The low-balance alert is a great idea as a backup, but you should be watching your checking account closely enough that you won't need the alert in the first place. Bank apps make monitoring your checking account easy, so get in the habit of checking yours at least a few times a week.

In addition to ensuring that you notice early if your account balance is moving in the wrong direction, frequently reviewing your account activity is also a great way to spot troublesome spending patterns, notice if you're getting caught in a Spending Rip Current, and Protect Monday Me.

> **KEY TAKEAWAYS**
>
> - Your checking account will be home base for your day-to-day financial life.
> - When you start earning money, set up a direct deposit to automatically move at least a portion of your paycheck straight into your checking account.
> - Linking your checking account to payment apps, like Zelle and Venmo, is a convenient way to pay for things. But monitor your account balance closely.

Now let's examine the less exciting but slightly more profitable way to keep your money in a bank: a savings account.

# 9

# *Savings Accounts*

Which would you prefer: a million dollars right now (*let me finish*), or a penny that doubles every day for a month? It sounds crazy, but that doubling penny will grow to more than $5,000,000 by day thirty. That's the power of *compounding*. As your investment earns money over time, your total amount goes up faster and faster because every dollar you earn begins earning money itself.

Sadly, a bank's savings account won't turn your penny into millions of dollars every month. If that were possible, I would've skipped the chapter on checking accounts. But a savings account will pay you interest on your money, and those earnings will compound. It probably won't make you rich, but a savings account is a valuable addition to your Money Toolkit. In this chapter, I'll suggest two reasons why having one is a smart financial move. Then I'll give you one reason why you'll eventually want to move at least some of your money from your traditional savings account into different types of investments.

First, though, let's review what a savings account is.

## What Is a Savings Account?

Here's how Northwestern University describes them: "Savings accounts are a way to put money aside for longer-term use than checking accounts. In return for 'lending' your money to the bank, savings accounts usually pay you a nominal amount of interest, which is an easy way to earn a few extra dollars over time."[1]

I noted earlier that checking accounts were historically described as *demand-deposit accounts* because you could start withdrawing your money as soon as you deposited it. That was the point of checking accounts: to create a financial home base where you could securely store money and use it to conveniently pay your regular expenses.

A savings account, on the other hand, was traditionally described as a *time deposit*. You'd commit your money to the bank for a period of time—say, one year—and the bank could earn a profit by lending your money out to other people (or businesses). The bank might charge a borrower 8 percent interest to use your money for that year, and then it could pay you 5 percent interest and still make a profit. If you think about it, there are two lenders in that situation: you loan your money to the bank, and the bank then loans your money to a borrower.

Savings accounts don't work exactly this way anymore. You can pull money out of a savings account much more easily now than in the past, although there are limits. For example, you can make only a certain number of withdrawals per month. Banks also typically demand that you keep a *minimum balance* (a minimum amount of money in your account) at all times. And while most savings accounts include an ATM card for withdrawing cash, they probably won't issue you a debit card that lets you spend everywhere.

In other words, savings accounts today now act like a combination of time and demand accounts. The banks clearly want you to keep at least a portion of your savings right where it is. But you don't have to lock all of it away with the bank for a minimum amount of time.

A true time-deposit account today has a new name: *certificate of deposit* (*CD*). With this account, you actually do commit your money for a specific time—three months, a year, three years. Because it knows it can lend out your money for that time, the bank will pay you a higher amount of interest for a CD than for a traditional savings account.

By the way, many checking accounts also require a minimum balance. But considering how awful their overdraft charges can be, you'll want to set your own minimum balance anyway, even if your checking account doesn't demand it.

Now let's talk about the benefits of savings accounts—followed by one big potential challenge with them.

---

**A savings account won't make you rich, but it will pay you a modest fee just for leaving your money parked there. It will also help you develop a saving habit and build a valuable "just in case" fund for Monday Me.**

---

## Cool Things about Savings Accounts

### 1. They pay you to save

Saving your money is like leaving a gift for your future self. It's also a great way to give your future self a financial safety net in case something comes up. More than a third of Americans say they don't have enough money stashed away to cover a $400 emergency, such as an unanticipated medical expense.[2] You don't want to live under that kind of financial stress.

Morgan Housel puts it well in his excellent book *The Psychology of Money*: "You don't need a specific reason to save. It's fine to save for a car, or a home, or for retirement. But it's equally important to save for things you can't possibly predict."[3] Monday Me will thank you. And as long as you're going to save, you might as well stash your money in a place that pays you to leave it there. Even with the modest interest rates most savings accounts pay, it'll be nice to earn some cash just for keeping your money about as safe as it could be.

**2. They help you build the saving habit**

One of the best reasons to have a savings account is that it gives you both a place and a process for putting away a portion of your money so you won't spend it. Saving money is a habit, just like spending is. So if you can build a habit of saving, you're less likely to be a person who spends without thinking—because those two habits are incompatible. Automatically depositing or transferring a portion of your paycheck into a savings account can make this process even easier. You'll also learn a valuable lesson most people never do: you can live on less of your money than you think.

The trick is to start building your money-saving muscles as early as possible. Get in the habit of sending a portion of all incoming money into a savings account where you'll be less tempted to pull it right back out again to buy stuff. You'll also have the fun of watching your savings grow over time.

# The One Drawback to Savings Accounts

## They Lose to Inflation

You've probably heard adults say things like, "When I was your age, a candy bar cost thirty cents" or "We used to be able to buy movie tickets for five dollars." We've all lived with this price-increase trend for so long that it seems normal. But it isn't. As technology improves and society becomes more prosperous, prices should be trending down over time. So why do the prices of so many things keep going up from generation to generation?

The real villain in this story is *inflation*: the expansion of the supply of money. As the government injects more dollars into the economy, all existing dollars—including the ones in your pocket or bank account right now—lose their buying power. Economists often describe this problem as *too many dollars chasing too few goods*.

Inflation represents the biggest drawback of a savings account—or, for that matter, keeping your money in an empty coffee can or under your mattress. As time goes by, inflation eats away at your dollars' power to buy stuff. If you leave all your money in a savings account earning 3 percent interest, but inflation is 4 percent, you're actually *losing* 1 percent of your money's real value every year.

That's why you'll want to set aside a portion of your money for investments that have the potential to earn more money than the moderate interest you'll make with a savings account. You'll want to find wealth-growing strategies that can out-earn inflation.

## Life Hack: Gamify Your Saving

Savings accounts are perfect for gamification. Set challenges for yourself. Try to save some amount by a specific date. Try to gradually put a higher and higher percentage of your paycheck right into savings.

If you're adding money regularly to your account, try not to look for a while and then guess how much you've saved.

## Life Hack: Look for a High-Interest Account

Banks want you to park your money with them. One way they compete for your business is to offer you the highest interest rates they can afford to pay on their savings accounts. So do your research and look for accounts with the best rates. You'll need to weigh the rates against other factors, though, such as the bank's reputation (check customer reviews online) and what other services they offer. You'll also want to figure out if using a particular bank will be convenient for you. For example, is their app user-friendly? Do they give you access to a lot of ATMs? You might be with a bank for years, so take your time with this decision.

## Life Hack: Use the Same Bank for Checking and Savings

Setting up checking and savings accounts with the same bank makes everything easier. You'll have one banking app that lets you see everything in one place—which will make it so much easier to keep track of your Whole Money Picture.

By doing your checking and savings with the same bank, you'll also find it more convenient to move money between accounts when you need to. For example, you can direct-deposit your entire paycheck into your checking account and then quickly transfer some of it to savings. You can even easily set an auto-transfer for a dollar amount or percentage of every paycheck from checking into savings. It's much easier to make these moves when you're keeping the money within the same bank than if you try to send it from one bank to another.

> **KEY TAKEAWAYS**
>
> - A savings account isn't the best wealth builder, but it will pay you just for keeping your money stored in a safe place.
> - One downside is that the interest rates savings accounts pay you are typically less than inflation, meaning the money you save there can still lose buying power.
> - Gamify your savings by setting challenges for yourself. Get creative and make saving fun.

Okay, now you know the basics of checking and savings accounts, two key tools in your Money Toolkit. Now let's talk about the tool you'll probably use for more transactions than any other: the credit card.

# 10

# *Credit Cards*

Hammers: Are they good or evil?

Ridiculous question, right? A hammer is morally neutral. It's just a tool. When someone uses it responsibly, a hammer can help build a home. But in the wrong hands? A murder weapon.

The story is similar to credit cards (minus the murder part). If you use them responsibly, they can make your daily life a lot more convenient. Also, the high *credit score* you can establish with responsible credit card use can help you build a strong financial reputation that will serve you well throughout your life. But use these little cards irresponsibly, and they can become a weapon of financial self-destruction.

So we'd better talk about them.

## What Is a Credit Card?

Bankrate.com describes a credit card as "A small revolving line of credit from an issuing bank."[1] But what the heck does that mean?

If you buy a T-shirt from a store, the product the store is selling you is obviously the shirt. But what about a loan? If you borrow money from a bank, what product is the bank selling you? Answer: money. Money is the product a lender sells. And just as the store needs to charge you more money for the shirt than they paid for it—otherwise their business doesn't earn a profit—a lender expects to be paid back with more money than they lend out. That's the role of *interest*: the amount of extra money a lender (like a credit card company) can charge you for letting you borrow their money.

A retailer might pay $9 for a T-shirt and then sell it to you for $14. In a similar way, a bank might borrow $1,000 at 3 percent interest and then loan it to you for a year and charge you 6 percent interest. At the end of that year, you'll have paid them back $1,060 for the privilege of using their money for the year. If every borrower behaves responsibly and repays their loans, the bank will earn $30 on every $1,000 it lends out.

Think of credit cards as little portable loans you can use anytime you want to buy stuff. When you use your card to pay for something, like dinner at a restaurant, the credit card company is making you a small loan. They'll pay for the dinner now, and a few weeks later they'll send you a bill for that meal and anything else you've *charged* (borrowed) on your credit card in the previous month.

Now comes the big decision: will you repay everything you've charged, or will you put off paying some or most of your *balance* (the total you owe) for another time? If you pay off the whole bill when it comes in, the credit card company doesn't charge you interest. Obviously, this is the smart choice. But if you choose to pay less than the full amount, the card company will start charging you interest on every dollar you roll over into the next bill. Do you really want to keep borrowing the money for that meal over and over, for months or even years—and eventually pay a lot more than the meal actually cost? That's what paying interest means.

## How Credit Cards Work

1. You apply for a credit card (an easy process), and the bank or credit card company sends you a little plastic card that has your name and a unique number on it. The card will come with a spending limit, maybe $2,000 or $3,000. (You can spend up to that amount using the card, and then you'll need to start paying it off before the card company lets you buy more things with it.)

2. You can start using the card right away to pay for just about anything, anywhere, including online. (You see the hammer metaphor here, right? Use it the right way, to buy only things you can afford, and the credit card is a very useful tool. But if you use it to overspend, making purchases without thinking about your Whole Money Picture or Monday Me, you could be doing the financial equivalent of smashing yourself over the head.)

3. At the end of a *billing cycle* (which is about a month), the card company will send you a bill for everything you've used the card to buy. That's called your *outstanding balance*: everything you owe the card company. They'll also give you options for how much to pay, from the whole amount (the money-savvy choice) all the way down to a minimum payment (the debt-digging option), usually just 1 percent or 2 percent of the total. If you pay off your bill 100 percent each month, you won't need to pay any interest charges for borrowing the money. But if you get in the habit of making only the minimum payment on your

credit card balance, you could be on your way to a years-long struggle of growing debt and massive financial stress.

---

**If you use it responsibly, your credit card can be a convenient tool. But that means paying your bill in full, every time. Never use your card to buy things you can't afford, and never roll your unpaid balance to the next bill.**

---

## How Do They Stay in Business?

The credit card is an incredibly convenient financial innovation. But it has a dark side, especially for young people just beginning to build their financial lives. Owning a credit card can create the feeling of having free money, because the card company doesn't demand you repay everything you borrow right away. And don't forget what you learned in Chapter 3 about how buying things with a credit card often doesn't even feel like spending money. That's because at the moment you make the purchase, you're actually not spending money—the credit card company is. Remember what that MIT study found: credit cards "disconnect the pleasure of buying with the pain of paying."[2]

Comedian Colin Jost captures this perfectly by describing how these companies keep finding ways to make buying easier and more fun: "Now they have credit cards you don't even have to swipe anymore. You can just wave them at stuff, like, *Weeee!* Just like they're little, tiny magic wands."[3]

When that first bill comes, new cardholders are often amazed at two things: how much money they've spent, and how forgiving the card company seems to be.

> New cardholder: *Whoa. How the heck did I spend $856 in my first month with this credit card? I don't have that kind of money.*
> Credit card company: *That's okay. You can pay us whatever portion you have. The minimum payment this month is only $17.*
> New cardholder: *Seriously? All you want right now is $17?*
> Credit card company: *Yep. And you still have more than $2,000 in available credit on the card, so you can keep spending.*
> New cardholder: *This is awesome. Thanks, Credit Card Company!*
> Credit card company: *Glad to have you as a customer.*
> New cardholder: [To himself] *$17? How do these fools stay in business?*

They're not fools. Let me show you how they stay in business.

## "Outstanding" Is Not a Compliment

Credit card companies earn most of their money in two ways.

### 1. Interest fees

This is credit card companies' biggest source of income—by far. In 2020, the credit card industry earned $76 billion in interest charges alone.[4]

Most people use their credit cards not as a tool of convenience but as a way to live more luxuriously than they can afford. They buy lots of stuff using their card, rack up a huge *outstanding balance*, and can't pay it off when the bill comes a month later. That's when the card company starts charging you *interest* to continue borrowing their money from one month to the next. The problem with living more luxuriously than you can afford today is that those interest charges are actually impoverishing Monday Me.

### 2. Interchange fees

Every time you buy something with a credit card, the card company charges the merchant a small transaction fee (usually about 1 percent to 3 percent of the total). If your restaurant meal costs $60 and you pay with a credit card, the card company might take $1.20 or so out of the total for processing the payment. These interchange fees are another big moneymaker for the credit card industry. In 2020, they accounted for $51 billion in card companies' income.[5]

The card companies also earn money by issuing cash advances (and earning interest on them) as well as charging penalties for things like late payments. Some card companies also charge customers an annual fee just to use their cards. But the vast majority of the industry's earnings comes from those two big sources: interest and transaction fees. And considering this is how they make most of their money, here's why credit cards should be a win-win-win for everybody.

## How We Should Use Credit Cards

Meet Chris. She just got her first credit card in the mail. She already has a checking account, with enough money in it to cover her regular expenses and give her a nice "just in case" cushion. So when her credit card bill comes, she knows she'll be able to use her checking account to pay it—and she'll always pay 100 percent of the bill. That way, she can use the card without worrying about getting stuck with interest charges.

Chris uses her credit card to pay for all sorts of things: groceries, gas for her car, phone bill, movie tickets, you name it. She even loads the credit card information into her Amazon account. When she wants to make a purchase online, she can do so in a few clicks.

But Chris has developed the right habits, and she makes the card work for her. She tracks her Whole Money Picture and always gives thought to Monday Me before buying anything. She even stops before every purchase to think it through and identify if what's driving her is an advertiser's message, peer pressure, or anything other than the benefit she'll get from the product itself.

Here's why this is a win-win-win.

**Chris wins**: She gets the convenience of paying for most of her day-to-day purchases easily, just by swiping, tapping, or waving her card. (*Weeee!*) And she rarely needs to carry cash or run to an ATM.

**The credit card company wins**: Chris pays off her bill in full every month, so the credit card company doesn't get to charge her interest. But every time Chris uses the card to buy something, the card company takes a processing fee. So they're still earning a nice little profit on Chris's card usage.

**The retailers win**: Some businesses complain about credit card company fees. But most know that without the ability to buy things using these cards, many of their customers wouldn't make the purchases at all. Businesses make many more sales because they allow their customers to use credit cards. Sharing a small portion of those profits with the card companies seems like a reasonable trade-off.

## How Millions of People Actually Use Credit Cards

Ah, if only everyone used their credit cards as responsibly as Chris does. The card companies would still earn tens of billions of dollars, sellers would still benefit enormously from their customers having such an easy way to buy from them, and we'd all enjoy the convenience of carrying around these handy little interest-free loan cards that let us pay for just about everything.

Unfortunately, that's not how many of us treat our credit cards. A study by the Federal Reserve found nearly half (47 percent) of US cardholders carry an outstanding balance from month to month.[6] And as we discussed earlier, one major study (by Discover Card) found that the average American in 2024 was $6,329 in credit card debt.[7] That's all pretty bad news. But you don't know just how bad until you realize the amount of interest those people are paying. The average credit card's interest rate in 2025 was about 24 percent.[8]

Let's imagine what this would mean for you if you were a typical cardholder with $6,329 in credit card debt. If your credit card had a 24 percent interest rate, and you paid only the minimum payment each month (let's say $150 per month, a little more than 2 percent of the balance), it would take you ninety-six months—eight years!—to pay it all off. That's because on top of paying for the $6,329 worth of stuff you actually bought, you'd also be paying another $8,010 in interest charges over that time.[9]

Think about that. Paying off a $6,329 credit card balance could cost you $8,010 just in interest payments. And what would you be getting for that additional $8,010? Not more stuff. Nothing, in fact, except the ability to keep not paying back the original $6,329. Another way to look at this: carrying that credit card debt for eight years basically means you'll be paying *twice* for everything you bought, plus another couple thousand bucks.

Oh, and want to hear something even crazier? If we drop your monthly payment from $150 down to $128 (which is about the 2 percent minimum the card company would allow), your repayment timeframe more than triples—from eight years to twenty-seven years! And you'd end up paying the card company more than $35,000 in interest payments.

Keep in mind, this all assumes you never spend another dollar on your credit card after your balance hits $6,329. Very few people stop spending as they get themselves into debt. So the situation is even worse than I'm describing here.

Nobody sums up this problem more eloquently than economist Bill Bonner: "When you owe money, it is often for things that no longer exist. Hamburgers eaten a month ago. Clothes that went out of style last summer. Ski vacations taken in last winter's snow. The pleasure may be long gone, but the discomfort of paying still lies ahead. With this burden of the past on your shoulders, you find it hard to move into the future. You shuffle along like a slave, forced to pay for yesterday's spending with tomorrow's work."[10]

## Your Balance Compounds Against You

Ben Franklin summed up the power of compounding nicely: "Money makes money. And the money that money makes, makes money."[11] But to understand the story from the credit card companies' perspective, we should listen to Albert Einstein, also a big fan of compounding: "Compound interest is the eighth wonder of the world. He who understands it, earns it. He who doesn't, pays it."[12] In other words, compounding is great when you're earning the gains; not so great when you're paying them. And with credit card debt, you're paying them.

When you use your credit card the right way, paying off your balance in full every month, the card will serve you well as a tool of real convenience. (*Yay, credit cards!*) But if you use it the wrong way, carrying a balance from month to month, the credit card companies are the ones enjoying the power of compounding interest—at your expense. The interest they charge you grows, which creates a bigger balance that you owe, which creates still more interest. (*Boo, credit cards!*)

# Life Hack: Pay Your Bill in Full—and Early

Paying off your credit card bill in full makes the card a great deal for you. It lets you use it to make purchases quickly and easily, and the money the card company loans you for the short term (just until the next bill comes) is actually free to borrow. No interest.

But here's another life hack: pay that bill as soon as it comes in. Don't wait until just before it's due. One of the nasty little secrets about credit cards is that if you miss one payment by even a day or two, the company can immediately and forever bump up your interest rate to the highest amount they can legally charge you. That could be as high as 30 percent. So pay it quickly, and pay it off completely. Every time.

> **KEY TAKEAWAYS**
>
> - A credit card can make your life a lot easier—but only if you pay off your entire bill and never leave an unpaid balance for the next month.
> - Monitor your credit card statement online, frequently, to make sure you're not spending so much that it could cause you trouble.
> - Pay your card bill as soon as you get it. That will minimize the chance that you miss a payment deadline, which could trigger penalties and higher interest charges.

Now you know the right way to use your credit card—so the credit card company isn't using *you*. As you develop these habits, you'll also establish a track record as someone who reliably pays their bills on time. And that will help you build one of the most important numbers in your financial life: your credit score. Let's talk about that.

# 11

# *Credit Scores*

I'm guessing one reason you're eager to finish school is that it means you'll finally be done with the endless testing, grading, and people making notes in your "permanent record" whenever you make a mistake. Unfortunately, that's not entirely the case.

We all have at least one big, ongoing exam that lasts our whole life. And yes, your grade on this forever test will include lots of time-sensitive homework assignments. It's called your *credit score*, and all sorts of organizations will be checking it throughout your life to decide whether they want to do business with you.

## What is a Credit Score?

Here's a definition from Equifax: "A credit score is a three-digit number, typically between 300 and 850, designed to represent your credit risk, or the likelihood you will pay your bills on time. Creditors and lenders consider your credit scores as one factor when deciding whether to approve you for a new account. Your credit scores may also impact the interest rate and other terms on any loan or other credit account for which you qualify."[1]

Think of your credit score as your financial good name. Maintaining a high score tells businesses that you're responsible, reliable, and that they can trust you to repay any money you borrow—on time, every time. Bottom line: building a high credit score can open up financial opportunities for you that aren't available to people with lower scores.

So, how do you build a high credit score? That's a little complicated. The credit scoring process is somewhat mysterious.

---

**Your credit score is one of the most important numbers in your financial life. It can determine whether you receive a loan and how much interest the lender charges you. It can even affect whether you can rent an apartment.**

---

## Finance Is So Weird

The first strange thing to note about your credit score is that it's based on a secret formula. The organizations that design the scoring systems treat their recipes as their private intellectual property, so they don't share the details of how they do it. That means nobody can tell you exactly what goes into your credit score or why your score is the exact number it is. (But there are big clues for how to build a high score, which we'll discuss below.)

The second bizarre thing about your credit score is that it's not just one score. There are three national credit-rating agencies—Equifax, Experian, and TransUnion—and they all build credit reports on all of us, which they summarize as three-digit scores. Then they sell our credit reports and credit scores to businesses, such as banks and mortgage companies, when we apply to those companies for loans.

Because each agency uses its own secret recipe, you will usually have three different credit scores at any time. When lenders check these scores as they evaluate whether to give you a loan, they'll usually take your middle score.

Here's the oddest thing of all. When a lender checks your credit scores—or, more accurately, when they pull your full *credit reports*—that act itself can knock down your scores a bit. Here's the logic behind this. If Lender D is reviewing your application for a loan or credit card, and they check your credit and find that you've just asked Lender C for money as well—and that you already have loans from Lenders A and B—they might find that a bit concerning. As Experian says, "It's a statistical fact that new debt raises the odds you'll fall behind on your old debts."[2]

But these drops are only temporary and decrease your score only a few points, so you don't need to worry much about a lender checking your credit. Still, this bizarre process—*look at my credit score, and it'll go down*—only adds to people's anxiety about having a business review their credit. The villain in *Avengers: Age of Ultron* nailed it: "Finance is so weird."[3]

## Why Is This Score So Important?

The credit-rating agencies will be documenting almost every big and small financial move you make—getting a new credit card, taking out a school loan, borrowing money for a car, and making your payments on time (or late). The agencies will analyze all these behaviors, run your history through their secret formula, and come up with your credit score.

This is why I said leaving school won't completely end your "permanent record" nightmares. As you enter adulthood, your credit history will become your new permanent record, your ongoing financial report card. And yes, everything will be graded: how well you handle debt, how much you owe, whether you take out too much credit at a given time, and how reliably and promptly you make your payments (which you can think of as your lifelong homework assignments).

The reason that both the score and your overall credit history matter is that businesses use this information as a key factor in deciding whether or not they want to work with you. Here are some of the businesses you can expect to pull your credit so they can learn more about you:

- **Lenders**

(When you apply for car loans, home mortgages, business loans, credit cards, and other types of loans.)

- **Landlords and property management companies**

(When you apply to rent an apartment or office space.)

- **Employers**

(When you apply for a job. Note: neither a potential employer nor your existing employer can actually see your *credit score*. But they can pull your credit report and see things like your outstanding debts, your track record of making payments, and if you've gotten into any serious money trouble, such as a bankruptcy.)

One big takeaway here is that maintaining a high credit score is important not only to help you qualify for loans and receive favorable terms on those loans. It can also play a big role in helping you get the apartment you want, the house you want, and even the jobs you want.

Or let's think about this the other way. Consider how many more obstacles you'll be creating for yourself if you neglect your financial responsibilities to the point that you develop a lousy credit report and low credit scores. Nobody wants to be that person. As the great comedian Dusty Slay puts it, "The best thing about having bad credit is not having to worry about identity theft."[4]

So let's quickly review how to keep your score high (and your identity worth stealing).

## The Not-So-Secret Secrets to a High Score

Let's turn to Equifax, one of the agencies that builds our credit reports and assigns us scores, for an overview of how they analyze our financial behavior. Here's a summary of what they say goes into our credit scores (which is similar to the other agencies' lists).[5]

- **Payment history**

This is the biggest single factor in your credit score. Lenders (not to mention your apartment's landlord) will want to know if you have a proven track record of making your payments on time. This shows not only your trustworthiness when it comes to repaying loans but also a general reliability and responsibility—traits your potential boss would also like to see.

- **Used credit vs. available credit**

Lenders also want to see how much of your spending limits you're actually using. If you have a credit card with a $10,000 limit, and you've racked up a $9,000 balance, that could lower your credit score. Lenders would prefer to see you using only about 30 percent of all your available credit. (Some quick definitions: *credit* means the amount of money you can borrow, like your spending limit on a credit card. *Debt* refers to the amount of money you've actually borrowed, like your outstanding balance on that credit card.)

- **Credit mix**

This refers to the fact that lenders prefer to see borrowers successfully managing different types of loans. In addition to a credit card (a *revolving loan*), they might be looking for *installment loans*, such as a mortgage or auto loan. (They're called installment loans because, unlike a revolving loan, you have a fixed amount to repay. After a certain number of payments, you've paid it off and the loan ends.)

- **Length of credit history**

Lenders will be looking at how long you've had your credit accounts as well as how well you've managed them. The longer you've been reliably making payments of all types, the better your score, and the more favorably lenders will view you.

- **New credit**

Lenders want to know if you've recently taken on more debt, like signing up for more credit cards or taking out new loans, and this could lower your score. Keeping your credit card accounts open long-term shows lenders you can maintain a good relationship with your creditors. Each time you sign up for new credit, that lowers the average time period of all your credit accounts. So you'll want to limit how many new accounts you open.

- **Hard inquiries**

Finally, here's that bizarre practice we discussed earlier, where lenders check your credit in response to your application for a loan or card— and that credit check lowers your score. Don't worry much about this, though. These so-called hard inquiries only ding your score a few points, and only for a few weeks. Also, if you're shopping around for a car loan and a bunch of lenders check your credit at the same time, that usually counts as just one hard inquiry.

## What's a Good Credit Score?

Credit scores range from 300 to 850. The average score in the United States is typically in the 705-to-720 range. Anything above 800 is considered excellent. Creditors view 740 to 799 as "very good" and from 670 to 739 as "good." Drop below 670, and you've got some work to do.

## Life Hack: Keep Your Accounts Active

Because one key to the mysterious credit score recipe is the length of your credit history, you'll want to keep your credit card accounts active for the long term. You shouldn't have much reason to cancel your cards anyway, unless you find it too difficult to have access to easy spending money. (And you're a money savvy teen, so that's not going to happen to you.)

## Life Hack: Don't Take On Too Much Credit

You should apply for a credit card if for no other reason than that it's an easy way to start building a credit history. In fact, you can also get a second card, and the rating agencies even suggest this, as long as you treat each card responsibly and pay both bills on time, every time.

Beyond a second credit card, though, you'll want to limit your credit to different types of accounts, such as a car loan or student loan.

# Life Hack: Check Your Credit Scores Regularly

Now that you know how big a role your credit score will play in your life, you can understand how important it is to make sure you're maintaining a high score (and if not, why not). So you'll want to review your credit reports and scores periodically. Also, these rating agencies make mistakes. Checking your reports regularly can help you catch errors so that you can ask the agencies to remove them.

The good news is you can check your own reports and scores for free once a year. As of 2025, the site to request them is AnnualCreditReport.com. Don't worry: checking your own credit is considered a "soft" inquiry and won't affect your score.

---

### KEY TAKEAWAYS

- A high credit score can open lots of doors for you, not just financially but also for things like renting an apartment and even getting a job.
- Open a credit card account and start using it as soon as you can. That's the first step to building your credit. But pay your bill off in full and pay it on time.
- Keep your credit card accounts active for as long as possible. This helps you grow your credit history, which brings up your score.

---

We've discussed credit cards and how the way you handle them affects your credit score. But you'll probably have another card in your pocket that lets you spend pretty much everywhere. Mishandling this card can create a different set of problems, so you'll need to learn some different strategies for handling it responsibly. So let's talk about debit cards.

# 12

# *Debit Cards*

## Would You Like Fees with That?

True story. An eighteen-year-old walked into a McDonald's and purchased an order of large fries and a drink. Total charge: $4.72. The problem was, she had only $1.68 in her checking account at the time. So when she paid with her debit card, that took her account below zero. The bank charged her a $35 overdraft fee immediately—and then kept charging her another $6 every day until her paycheck hit the account.[1] *Total*, total charge for that drink and fries: $71. I hope it was delicious.

In one important way, a debit card makes it easier than a credit card to keep your spending under control. Because it pulls directly from your checking account (or if you choose, your savings account), a debit card won't give you the opportunity to run up massive debt the way you can with a credit card. If you drain your account down to zero and keep spending, your bank will eventually stop paying for your purchases and start declining them. And if you don't have overdraft protection, they might decline any purchase you try to make that takes your account below zero.

When you overspend on your credit card, you create a long-term problem: your outstanding balance grows, the card company hits you with high interest charges, and that makes your balance grow even more. That's a big problem for Monday Me. But when you overspend using a debit card, you can create a lot of right-now problems for Today Me. So let's talk about it.

## What Is a Debit Card?

Here's a useful definition from NerdWallet: "A debit card is a payment card that lets you make secure purchases online and in person by drawing money directly from your checking account. You're not borrowing from a line of credit like you would with a credit card or a 'buy now, pay later' service; the money on your debit card pulls from your own money as you spend."[2]

You can use a debit card pretty much everywhere that takes a credit card. You might find it a little less convenient to use a debit card, because you'll often have to enter your *PIN (Personal Identification Number)* to complete the transaction. But hey, if that extra step slows down an online purchase long enough for your rational mind to figure out that—*Wait a minute!*—you're just buying for the quick rush of endorphins, then maybe that can save you from wasting your money and buying Tomorrow's Junk.

---

**A debit card gives you the same electronic-payment conveniences that you get with a credit card. And by pulling money right from your bank account to pay for your purchases, the debit card limits your ability to overspend.**

---

## Cool Things about Debit Cards

1. **They limit your spending**

Debit cards give you the same convenience as credit cards in letting you pay for things anywhere, but without the same opportunity to spend yourself thousands of dollars into debt. For that benefit alone, limiting your ability to drown in a Spending Rip Current, a debit card can be an invaluable tool in your Money Toolkit.

2. **They can help you avoid merchant fees**

In Chapter 10, I mentioned that one way credit card companies earn money is by charging businesses a processing fee every time their customers pay with a credit card. And while most businesses pay these transaction fees themselves, some try to pass the costs onto you by adding an extra charge if you pay by credit card. Because those businesses don't get hit with a processing fee for debit card payments, you can avoid those charges when you use your debit card.

3. **They let you grab cash from ATMs**

Debit cards also double as ATM cards, so you can use them at these machines to pull money out of your checking account. Just remember to use only ATMs that are part of your bank's network, because those transactions are free. If you use a debit card to grab cash out of an ATM not affiliated with your bank, those transactions can be $5 or more. Kind of crazy to pay a $5 fee just to pull out $20 of your own money. So plan ahead. If you're going to need cash, stop by one of your bank's ATMs.

## Risks of Mismanaging Your Debit Card

1. **Overdraft fees**

We reviewed overdrafts in the checking account chapter, but it's worth repeating, because it's easy to fall into this trap. In fact, US government data from the end of 2023 showed that more than one in four households had paid a fee in the previous year for either an overdraft or *non-sufficient funds* (the same thing, basically).³ With a little effort, these charges are entirely avoidable. But if you're not monitoring your checking account balance and use your debit card to pay for something that costs more than you have in the account, you could find yourself buying a fast-food meal with a side of fees.

### 2. Penalties from other businesses

In addition to the overdraft fees your bank charges you, misusing your debit card can create another big problem, one that can even pull down your credit score. Let's say you spend carelessly with your debit card for a few days, buying new clothes, and that takes your balance down to $300. You also have an automatic payment scheduled soon for your car loan, which is $500 a month.

Those clothes you paid for with your debit card won't trigger an overdraft charge, because you did keep $300 in the account. But those purchases will take your balance low enough that when the bank reaches into your account for the $500 car payment, that will cause an overdraft fee. That's problem number one. Problem number two is that now you've missed a car payment. That can create all sorts of problems with your auto lender, including penalties for a late payment. They might even add the missed payment to your credit report, which will lower your credit score.

### 3. They don't offer as much fraud protection as credit cards do

If someone steals your credit card (or you lose it and someone finds it), you won't be held responsible for any charges the lowlife makes with it. Federal law offers a lot of protection for credit card owners. But debit cards? A different story.

If you call your bank and report your debit card stolen within two days—and there are already fraudulent charges on it—your bank is limited by law to charging you only $50 of the amount stolen. They have to repay your account for whatever else the thief charged. If you wait between three and sixty days to file the report, the bank could hold you responsible for as much as $500 of the lowlife's illegal purchases. Wait more than sixty days, in fact, and you could lose all your stolen money.[4]

People have had their checking accounts completely drained this way. That's why the most important safeguards, the ones every cybersecurity professional tells consumers, are never to share your PIN with anyone and to shop online only at trusted sites.

## Life Hack: Build Your Just-In-Case Cushion

To get all the conveniences of using a debit card without the risks of overspending and penalty fees, make sure you have enough money in your checking account so that you won't accidentally make a debit card purchase that takes your account below zero. Build a just-in-case cushion, and never let your account fall below that amount.

## Life Hack: Keep on Checking

If you're developing the habit of tracking your Whole Money Picture, this will become a natural part of your financial routine. Monitor your checking account frequently enough that you always have a good idea of how much money is in there. Banks make this easy today with apps that let you check your balance and all transactions anytime.

And to repeat a life hack from a previous chapter: add your regular auto-payments to your calendar. That way, you'll always know if a business you buy from—Netflix, Apple, your auto lender, your apartment's property management company—is about to pull a monthly payment from your account. When you know that you'll be much less likely to make a mistaken debit card purchase that could take your account negative.

It's called your checking account. Make sure you're checking it.

---

**KEY TAKEAWAYS**

- A debit card is a great way to get the purchasing convenience of a credit card without the risk of spending yourself into long-term debt.

- Use your debit card to access cash, but only at ATMs affiliated with your bank. Those withdrawals should be free. Other banks' ATMs charge high fees.

- Review your checking account frequently so you know how much is there. This will reduce the chances of a debit card purchase that triggers an overdraft.

---

We've talked a lot about the fun side of your Money Toolkit—using your tools to buy stuff. Now let's talk about what happens after the buying. In the next chapter, we'll discuss paying bills.

# 13

# *Bills*

> I love paying bills.
>
> Nobody, Ever

Jerry Seinfeld has a funny bit about how illogical it is that restaurants wait until after you've finished eating to bring you the bill. "First of all, when you're really full, you can't remember being hungry ever in your life." Obviously, when the meal is over, you're no longer excited about eating, so you're definitely not going to be excited about getting the bill. So, Seinfeld says, that might not be the best time to ask for payment. "We're not hungry now. Why are we buying all this food?"[1]

Interesting insight. But I think there's a simpler reason that restaurant customers don't like receiving the bill after their meal. People hate paying bills, period. I'm guessing you've never heard anybody say, "What's great about McDonald's is that they make you pay before they give you the food. I'm lovin' it!" People eating at a restaurant wouldn't enjoy handing over their money first, either.

A 2021 study found that Americans rank paying bills among their most hated administrative tasks. For context, here's what else was on that list: cleaning the house, renewing a driver's license, and doing taxes.[2] Paying bills today is easier than ever. Most businesses let you pay online. Many even let you make payments automatically, which means you don't need to do anything. Cleaning your house still takes a lot of effort. So does completing a tax return. But paying bills has gotten far easier and less time-consuming in recent years. So why do people still rank it alongside mopping floors and filling out IRS forms? I'm going to offer an unpopular explanation below. First, though, let's define our term.

## What Is a Bill?

The Cambridge Dictionary defines a bill this way: "A request for payment of money owed, or the piece of paper on which it is written."[3]

Pretty straightforward, right? You receive some product or service, and the company asks you for payment. So why do so many people complain about it?

I think the universal hatred of bill-paying comes down to one thing: most people have an unhealthy relationship with money. They spend without regard to their Whole Money Picture, get caught in Spending Rip Currents, and find themselves stuck with a lot of Tomorrow's Junk. When the businesses that sold them all this stuff ask for payment, these people either don't have enough money to pay the bill, or they do, but they're horrified to discover how much they've spent. And like shooting the messenger, these people blame the businesses they bought from, rather than their own careless spending, for the financial mess that the bills create.

So here's my unpopular opinion.

**If you develop a healthy relationship with money and a smart financial routine, you might actually enjoy paying your bills.**

## Paying Bills Should Feel Great

You're becoming a money savvy teen, which means you're learning how to develop a healthy relationship with money. That includes learning how to appreciate the entire process of interacting with your money, including paying for the stuff you buy. Here's why bill-paying should feel great.

- **You'll know you're a full player in the economy**

You get to choose how and where you spend your money—which companies earn your business and which don't. When you pay your bills, you're exercising your right as an independent actor, a full-fledged participant in the economy.

- **You'll be strengthening your credit score**

Every bill you pay in full and on time helps to strengthen your credit score and improve your overall credit history. Remember, a strong credit history can open doors for you throughout your life. It might help you qualify for the best loans, rent an apartment, and even land the job you want.

- **You'll know you're doing the responsible thing**

Paying bills is a very grown-up thing to do. But sadly, even many adults don't pay their bills reliably. A 2024 study found that 37 percent of Americans had been charged a late fee within the previous year for missing some type of payment—a credit card bill, utilities for their home, or even rent.[4] In addition to avoiding late charges, paying your bills on time can also earn you a sense of pride as a mature, responsible person, because you'll know you're holding up your end of the deal.

I wasn't entirely serious with the quote at the beginning of this chapter when I suggested that *Nobody, Ever* said they love paying bills. I've said it myself many times (often to understandable eye rolls from my wife and daughter). And for the reasons we've just discussed, I'm hoping you'll learn to love paying bills, too.

With that in mind, here are some strategies to make bill-paying easier and more convenient.

## Life Hack: Set It but Don't Forget It

Automate every recurring expense you can. It's a great way to protect against missing a payment because you forgot, or the business's email got caught in your spam folder, or a zillion other possible reasons. When you sign up for a new subscription or any type of ongoing service (Netflix, your internet service provider, your car loan, etc.), choose the automatic-payment option if it's available. You can have your payments put on your credit card or deducted right from your checking account. Just remember that if you're auto-paying businesses right from your bank account, you'll need to add a little cushion to your balance.

Also, even for your automatic payments, you'll want to review your bills each time. Businesses make mistakes. So do a quick scan of each new bill to make sure everything looks right.

## Life Hack: Make an Event Out of It

We discussed this in the checking account chapter, but it's worth repeating. Whether you're paying automatically or manually, I'd suggest creating a calendar event for each recurring bill. That way, you'll have one place to look for your ongoing payments, and you'll get into the habit of checking your calendar to see what bills you have coming up. (Great way to monitor your Whole Money Picture.)

Businesses that bill monthly usually send their bills around the same time each month. So figure out when that is for each recurring bill, and add the payment as an event on your calendar app. If you have to manually pay some bills online or by check, rather than automatically, I'd also suggest setting those calendar events at least a week earlier than their due date. Better to pay a bill early than late.

As for what the event should look like, my wife Julie suggests four things in the title line, the key details you'll see when you review your calendar's events for the day.

1) Business name

2) Automatic or manual payment

3) Source of the payment (your credit card, your checking account)

4) Amount (or a rough guess)

Let's say you have automatic payments set for your Netflix account and you put the charge on your credit card. And let's say it costs you about $20 a month. Here's what your calendar event might look like: **Netflix: Auto: CC: $20.**

Maybe you also pay your own health insurance, and the insurer doesn't allow you to put the charge on your credit card or to schedule an auto-pay service. So you'll need to go into your insurance account each month and pay online, pulling the money from your checking account. That calendar event might look like this: **XYZ Insur: Manual: CHKG: $430.**

Soon, you'll get very good at knowing which bills get paid on which days, and which of your Money Tools you use to pay each of them. At that point, you can even make this a game. Open your calendar app, hand your phone to a friend, and ask them to test you. *What date does Netflix get paid? Where does the money come from to make your insurance payment?* That type of thing.

I told you paying bills is awesome.

> **KEY TAKEAWAYS**
> 
> - If you develop a healthy relationship with money, paying your bills can be a great feeling—earning you a sense of responsibility and pride.
> 
> - Pay your bills early. That's the best way to ensure you don't risk penalties, damage to your credit score, and the other problems of paying bills late.
> 
> - Automate bill payments whenever possible—but make sure you're still reviewing each bill, because businesses make mistakes.

Okay, we've squeezed about as much fun as possible out of a chapter on paying bills. But in the next chapter, the fun should come a lot more naturally. We'll be discussing everybody's favorite money-management topic: budgets.

# 14

# *Budgets*

Let's hear from Jerry Seinfeld one more time. There's a scene in the sitcom *Seinfeld* where Jerry goes to a car rental place to pick up a midsize car he's reserved. The woman behind the counter tells him they're out of midsize cars. That begins a great back-and-forth where she defends the fact that they've run out of cars and Jerry insists his reservation is supposed to keep that very thing from happening.

"See, you know how to take the reservation. You just don't know how to *hold* the reservation. And that's really the most important part of the reservation—the holding. Anybody can just take them."[1]

What does this have to do with budgets?

The good news is the vast majority of adults (about 90 percent, according to a 2024 survey) say they try to budget their money.[2] The bad news? About 84 percent of those who have a monthly budget say they overspend anyway.[3] "Creating a budget (and sticking to it) is one of the most important things you can do to improve your financial situation," say the financial planners at Chatterton & Associates.[4] It seems most people can manage the "creating" part of their budgets, just not the "sticking to it" part. And as Jerry Seinfeld might put it: *That's really the most important part of the budget—the sticking to it. Anybody can just create them.*

Actually, I think simply creating a budget can deliver big financial benefits all by itself. We'll talk about that below. First, though, let's define our term.

## What Is a Budget?

From Yale University: "A budget is a way to keep track of the money you are getting and the money you are spending. A budget is a great way to make sure that you can cover your expenses from month to month."[5]

Yale's definition is true as far as it goes. But I'd argue you can do a lot more with a budget than just cover your monthly expenses. When you write out this simple plan to manage your money, a lot of the principles you've learned in this book start falling into place. For example, a budget can help you:

- **Monitor Your Whole Money Picture**
- **Protect Monday Me**
- **Avoid the Spending Rip Current**
- **Prevent a Lot of Tomorrow's Junk purchases**
- **Dodge the Ad Barrage** (*Nice try, advertisers, but it's just not in my budget this month.*)
- **Take an Aerial View of Your Finances**

Another way to think about this is that your budget *is* your Whole Money Picture. When you can see at a glance how much money you have coming in, how much you have going out, and exactly how you're spending every dollar, it will become much more difficult to make the careless decisions that get millions of adults into financial trouble. Pretty impressive for a Money Tool so simple it could fit on half a sheet of paper.

A budget is the tool in your Money Toolkit that helps you manage all the other tools. It can help you protect and grow your bank accounts, pay bills on time, control your spending, and build a better credit score.

## Did You Write Your Budget with a Magic Wand?

In the chapter on advertising, we talked about the value of reasoning through a possible purchase before you hand over your money. When you force yourself to talk through why you want the item—and the trick is to do this *out loud*—you'll often discover what's driving you isn't the product itself but rather an effective advertising message. (Or it could be boredom or your brain's craving for a quick rush of feel-good hormones.) By stopping to check with the rational centers of your brain, you're essentially breaking a spell that might otherwise have you spending your money almost unconsciously. That simple process can save you money, prevent a lot of Tomorrow's Junk, and protect you against the constant stress of growing debt.

There's a similar principle at work when you write out a budget. Just by forcing yourself to take a close look at how much money you're bringing in, how much you're sending out, and where it's all going, you can uncover unhealthy money habits and begin to correct them. So although I agree that sticking to your budget is an invaluable step toward smart money management, I also think a lot of a budget's magic comes from simply creating and looking at it.

## Lots of Ways to Budget

Creating a budget is easy and shouldn't take you more than a few minutes. And because it's such a valuable money tool, a lot of smart people have devised clever strategies to make it even easier. Here are a few ways to build a budget.

### 1. The traditional method

Can't get much simpler than this. Just write out your income (each source and your expected total) on one side and then your anticipated expenses on the other. You can also break down your expenses into needs and wants, or fixed and variable expenses.

As you write all this out, you'll get a sense of how much you can afford to spend on your variable expenses and wants—things like entertainment. And you'll always want to set aside some money in your budget for *savings*, so that should have its own line on the budget.

| SAMPLE MONTHLY BUDGET | | | |
|---|---|---|---|
| *Income* | | *Expenses* | |
| | | (Fixed) | |
| Job | $4,000 | Rent | −$2,000 |
| Side hustle | $1,000 | Phone | −$80 |
| Gifts | $75 | Groceries | −$300 |
| Allowance | $100 | Car Payment | −$300 |
| **TOTAL** | **$5,175** | Savings | −$1,000 |
| | | (Variable) | |
| | | Entertainment | −$400 |
| | | Clothes | −$150 |
| | | Meals Out | −$400 |
| | | **TOTAL** | **−$4,630** |

*Note*: In this case, even after meeting your $1,000 monthly saving goal, you'll still have cash left over each month for unplanned expenses, a vacation fund, or even investments.

2. **The envelope method**

This budgeting strategy started back in the Paleolithic Era when I was your age, but it's still popular today. The process is simple: you set up envelopes for all categories of spending you plan for the month and then stuff each envelope with as much cash as you've budgeted for that category.

In my ancient generation, we set up budget envelopes for things like food, cave decorations, dinosaur-repellant spray, and fire-making tools. But we live in the modern era now, and you'll probably want envelopes for spending on dinners out, clothing, and movies. The idea is, if you find your movies envelope empty in the middle of the month, sorry, no more trips to the movie theater until the following month.

You can use this budgeting approach without physical envelopes. Many budgeting apps let you create digital spending categories, allocate specific amounts of money to them, and then monitor the money left in each category as the month progresses. Some apps let you set up alerts to let you know when a digital "envelope" falls below a specific dollar amount.

3. **Proportional budgeting**

With this strategy, you'll allocate a percentage of your income into broad buckets for spending. One common formula is the 50-30-20 strategy. This forces you to allocate 50 percent of your spending to "needs" (rent, student loan payments), 30 percent for "wants" (meals out, cave decorations), and 20 percent for savings. As your needs or goals change, you can easily adjust these percentages from month to month.

# Life Hack: Make Saving Automatic

In his excellent book *The Latte Factor*, David Bach correctly points out that most people have difficulty saving, even if they write it into their budget. Every month, there will be something they'd rather do with that money than deposit it into their savings account.

So he suggests making that payment—a payment to yourself, essentially—automatic. "Take the day-to-day decision out of your hands by setting up a simple, automatic system that will run all by itself in the unseen background. So it takes zero discipline, zero self-control, zero willpower. Just set it up and let it run."[6]

## Life Hack: Gamify Your Budgets

Make budgeting an ongoing game. Did you manage to keep your "wants" spending to just 30 percent of your income for a couple of months in a row? Great. Now level up and try to get that number down to 20 percent. Or aim to increase your monthly savings allocation every few months—from 20 percent to 25 percent to 30 percent and so on.

> ### KEY TAKEAWAYS
>
> - A budget is the tool in your Money Toolkit that can help you more successfully manage all the other tools—including bills, credit cards, and savings accounts.
> - You can benefit greatly just by writing out a budget and examining it, because it can help you uncover a lot of poor spending decisions.
> - Always allocate a portion of your budget to savings—and automate those payments to yourself, so they don't require a conscious decision each time.

When you've built the habit of budgeting your money, sticking to your budgets, and always sending some of your income into savings, you'll soon find yourself piling up cash for your future. And you'll want to move at least some of that cash into something with greater earning potential than your savings account. So let's talk about investing.

# 15

# *Investments*

A financial advisor once told me about an ingenious scam in her profession. Here's how it works. Imagine a wealth manager (someone who handles rich people's investments) trying to find new clients. He rents a list of 50,000 wealthy people's email addresses and sends the following message to half of them. *I've been researching XYZ Company, and they're doing some amazing things. I'm confident the company's stock will be up this time next week.*

To the other half, he sends this: *I've been researching XYZ Company, and they're making some disastrous decisions. I'm confident the company's stock will be* down *this time next week.*

A week later, XYZ's stock is up. So our wealth manager tosses the 25,000 addresses that received his "stock will be down" message. (No point in emailing them again.) For the 25,000 who saw him get his first prediction "right," he drafts two new messages: *ABC Company's stock will be higher,* and *ABC Company's stock will be lower.* Then he sends each version of that email to 12,500 addresses. He keeps doing this every week. After about a month, thousands of people will have seen this wealth manager make "correct" stock predictions four or five times in a row. Some will probably hire him to invest their money.

My point with this story isn't to scare you away from investing or to suggest that the typical wealth manager isn't honest or ethical. (Most are.) It's only to show you how easily people, even smart people, can be fooled when someone promises to make them money quickly and easily. Your parents are right: if something sounds too good to be true, hide your wallet.

Investing the right way has a long track record of helping millions of people build wealth. But the key is doing it the right way. When it comes to investing, you'll encounter opportunities everywhere to do it the wrong way. So let's talk about it.

## What Is an Investment?

Here's a great definition from Axis Max Life Insurance: "An investment can be defined as an asset that is created with the intention of helping your wealth to grow with time and secure your future financial requirements."[1]

Investing can get very technical, but the concept is simple. You take a portion of your money and place it in an asset: a bond, a business's stock, a fund comprised of many stocks, a piece of real estate. Gaining the use of your money helps the asset increase its value over time. When you buy a few shares of Amazon stock, the company's value goes up a little. That means Amazon can raise a little more cash to build warehouses or to finally develop an algorithm that can deliver us the stuff we want before we have to ask. (*I'm still waiting, Amazon.*) As the asset grows in value, so does the value of your investment—so you make money.

## Flipping a Coin?

Some people say investing is no different from gambling. Using the broadest definition of a gamble—taking an action with a risk of loss—that's true. But then so is playing any sport (*They beat us*), trying a new food for the first time (*Yuck. People pay to eat this?*), or just stepping out of the shower. (*Help!*) Life is one long series of actions that carry a risk of loss. (And at the end, the absolute certainty of it. Maybe even from stepping out of the shower.)

But if we use the definition these people actually mean when they try to equate investing with gambling—*a game of chance for money*—then we can see where their logic fails.

First of all, unless you're cheating, gambling is usually a game of luck. Flip the coin, pull the slot machine's handle, pick a card—winning is a matter of pure chance.

Second, gambling is a *zero-sum* game. For you to win money, the casino needs to lose money. You can't have poker night with your friends where all the players come away with more money than they brought to the game. In gambling, someone is always going to lose.

And third, when you gamble against professionals—casinos, online poker companies—those organizations will always tilt the odds in their favor. So you'll always have a greater chance of losing than of winning.

None of this is true about investing.

Although there's always a risk of loss, most investments you'll make will be in assets or businesses that already have some value. (By contrast, there's no intrinsic value in the number six on the casino's roulette table.) The businesses you invest in will be trying to grow and become more successful. And gaining access to your money will actually improve the odds of that happening. There will be some luck in the outcome, of course, but this isn't a game of pure chance.

Investing also isn't a zero-sum game. If all goes according to plan, your investment will create wealth for both you and the asset itself. You can both win. Not true at the blackjack table.

And finally, with smart, thoughtful investing, the odds are actually in your favor. As I'll show you below, stock values tend to go up over time. Staying in these investments increases your chances of building wealth. But do you know what mathematicians say about gambling at a casino? Every additional time you play, the odds decrease that you'll come out ahead.

---

The safest, most proven way to invest your way to wealth is to do it slowly, using boring investments and the power of compounding.

---

## Investing Is Awesome

If you invest thoughtfully and patiently, the odds are in your favor that you'll grow your wealth over time. So why would I start this chapter with a story about an investment scam? Because most people don't want to invest thoughtfully and patiently. They want to make lots of money *right now*. It's human nature to be impatient for the things we want and to make emotional rather than logical decisions to try to get those things. On the website of his money-management company The Bahnsen Group, author and financial advisor David Bahnsen explains the challenge perfectly: "Human nature is the enemy of success, yet all investors are humans. The behavioral decisions one makes—often decisions to *not do something*—will consistently trump individual portfolio selections when it comes to achieving a financial objective."[2]

In other words, behave logically and use reason and patience—not your emotions—to evaluate investment decisions. Let these be your guiding investment principles. When you're making decisions about how and where to invest your money, make sure you're listening to these principles. In fact, turn their volume way up, so they can drown out the scammers, liars, and cheats coming at you with promises to *Double your money in three months!* or, *Get crypto-rich now!* or, *Build a multimillion-dollar business in your pajamas with four easy steps!*

If you can train yourself to avoid these tempting promises to get rich quick, you'll greatly increase your chances of investment success. With that in mind, let's review what makes investing awesome—and when to hide your wallet.

## Cool Things about Investing

### 1. It helps you build wealth

Every investment carries at least some risk. And you definitely need to be careful with those ultra-exciting opportunities, like the latest cryptocurrencies. (Those "investments" actually *are* like flipping a coin—a digital coin.) But when you invest in the big, boring assets, and keep your money there for the long term, the odds are high that you'll grow your wealth. As Nobel Prize-winning economist Paul Samuelson says, "Investing should be more like watching paint dry or watching grass grow. If you want excitement, take $800 and go to Las Vegas."[3]

Here's a great example. Investopedia reviewed the history of the S&P 500. That's just a big basket of stocks of the 500 leading US companies, all rolled into one investment. When you buy into it, you're essentially buying a tiny (*tiny, tiny*) portion of all the companies in the index. No big bet on one exciting tech or media company. It's as though you're just investing in the US economy as a whole. Sounds pretty boring, right? But between 1928 and 2024, the S&P 500's investors earned an average of 10 percent per year.[4] And oh, the fun you could have with those gains!

In case you're wondering, Investopedia's research also takes *inflation* into account over that time. Even accounting for how much inflation ate away at the dollar's value, the average yearly gain was still nearly 7 percent. To give you an idea of what that means, imagine putting $5,000 into a simple investment that earns an average of 7 percent a year and leaving it there for thirty years. It's just sitting there, but it's growing. In fact, it's *compounding*, because your money earns money and then that money earns money itself, and so on. After thirty years, your investment is worth $38,061—almost eight times what you put in. And you never had to add another dollar to it.

As Morgan Housel writes in *The Psychology of Money*, "Good investing isn't necessarily about earning the highest returns, because the highest returns need to be one-off hits that can't be repeated. It's about earning pretty good returns that you can stick with and that can be repeated for the longest period of time. That's when compounding runs wild."[5]

### 2. It keeps money out of the Spending Rip Current

When I asked Certified Public Accountant Jerry Markell for his take on this, he had a brilliant response: "Happiness is not for sale. When you try to purchase it today with consumer products, you're devastating your financial future and well-being."

Every dollar you invest is more than just a chance to do something productive in the world and earn yourself some money in return—although it is those things as well. It's also a dollar that can't get washed away in a Spending Rip Current or wasted on Tomorrow's Junk, and it's a dollar no advertisers can get their hands on.

Setting aside a portion of your money for investments is one of the best things you can do for Monday Me—and for Next Decade Me.

3. **It helps you stay ahead of inflation**

When financial professionals say there's risk in every investment, they don't mean only that you might not earn money. They also mean you could lose a portion of the investment itself—or all of it. But the truth is, anything you do with your money carries risk in one form or another. When you keep money in a savings account, you don't have much risk of losing it. (While banks do fail, the government insures accounts up to $250,000.) But if the bank isn't paying you more in interest than you're losing to inflation, that savings account could still be eroding your wealth. Putting your money in a shoebox and hiding it under your bed carries the same inflation risk. In fact, that strategy could be worse, because your shoebox won't pay you interest like your savings account will.

One of the virtues of placing your money in assets like stocks, funds, or real estate is that those assets tend to grow at a faster pace than inflation. So over time, keeping your money invested will give you a better chance to build wealth in the actual dollar amounts that will still translate to real wealth years down the road when you're ready to cash in your investments.

# Investment Red Flags to Watch Out For

1. **It's "exciting"**

Have your friends told you about some new crypto coin they've invested in? Are they making money on it? Great. But instead of taking their advice to pour your money into it, offer them some advice instead: cash out.

If an investment opportunity is getting buzz, that means the people chasing the get-rich-quick opportunities are pouring their money into it. And that often means the people who set up the investment are going to take advantage of its now higher price and cash out their own money. Then the price will fall, and the late-to-the-game people will lose their investments. That's why professional investors often describe these amateurs as "the dumb money."

2. It's "easy money"

The *process* of investing can be easy. You buy an index fund (like the S&P 500) and let your investment money sit there and compound. But actually making money on newer or smaller investments, like a hot tech stock everybody's talking about on social media or your friend's plan to buy laundromats, won't be easy.

If anyone tells you their investment plan will deliver "easy" success, unless they're talking about the very passive and very boring methods of long-term stock or fund investing, they're probably wrong (or worse, lying to you).

3. It "can't lose"

Yes, it can.

If someone offers you an opportunity to buy into an investment that's "a sure thing" or "can't lose," hide your wallet.

## Life Hack: Keep It Boring

Exciting new investing opportunities like cryptocurrencies grab headlines. But what happens if the early investors in these coins, the ones who now have millions and even billions of dollars' worth of them, decide to cash out? Those who invested much later, and at much higher prices, could lose a lot of their money. In fact, this happens every day to those chasing get-rich-quick opportunities like the latest crypto fad or some hot AI tech startup.

Your chances of investment success will be higher if you're willing to make investments that don't sound exciting, don't go up and down like crazy, and don't get much buzz. Keep it boring. Invest in quality businesses and assets. Then let the power of time and compounding work for you.

> **KEY TAKEAWAYS**
>
> - Three of the most valuable traits you can bring to your investments are logic, thoughtfulness, and patience.
> - If someone tells you an investment opportunity can't lose, or that success will be easy, run the other way.
> - Investment success tends to come from boring, long-term financial moves. Let your investments be boring—and find your excitement elsewhere.

Okay, we've reviewed all the basic tools in your Money Toolkit and discussed how to use them properly. In this part's final chapter, I'm going to show you some examples of how high-profile people used these tools improperly—and what those missteps cost them.

# 16

# *The Costs of Mismanaging Your Money Toolkit*

Time for another true story. A man in England tried to rob a bank by walking up to the counter and handing the teller a note demanding all the cash in the drawer. But the handwriting was so sloppy that the teller couldn't read the note. After what must have been a very awkward few minutes, the would-be robber ran out of the bank. Then, incredibly, he tried the same stunt again at two more banks. His second attempt also failed, for the same reason. (Bank teller: *I'm sorry; I don't know what this says. What are you asking me here, Sir? Sir, where are you going?*) On his third attempt, he actually managed to get away with a small amount of money. But the criminal mastermind lasted only a few hours on the street before the police caught him.[1]

The point? When it comes to money, everybody makes mistakes. Smart, dumb, poor, rich, bank robber—everybody.

You, too, are going to make mistakes with your money. The goal is to limit the number of these mistakes and keep them from becoming a pattern, so they don't have a chance to bring down your entire financial house.

Speaking of which, let's review a few real-world stories of wealthy celebrities who mishandled some part of their Money Toolkits—and lost a fortune as a result. The purpose of this chapter isn't to criticize anyone. I just want to show you that although mistakes are a natural part of life, you can't afford to let poor money management become a part of *your* life.

## Celebrity Financial Horror Story: Kevin Bacon and Kyra Sedgwick

### (Mismanaged Money Tool: Investments)

Married couple and longtime film actors Kevin Bacon and Kyra Sedgwick amassed a fortune estimated at tens of millions of dollars. But they entrusted a major portion of their wealth to an investment manager named Bernie Madoff.

Years later, the world discovered Madoff was running a massive criminal scheme and defrauding his clients. Madoff's decades-long scam destroyed thousands of people's life savings and cost this celebrity couple millions of dollars. As Bacon later said, "We had most of our money in Madoff."[2]

## Life Hack: Don't Take Shortcuts with Your Investments

Bacon humbly explained the lesson he learned in an interview: "If something is too good to be true, it's too good to be true."[3]

You're going to make mistakes with your money. That's part of life. The key is not to let any of those mistakes become patterns.

# Celebrity Financial Horror Story: Johnny Depp

## (Mismanaged Money Tool: Savings)

Despite earning an estimated $650 million from his movies, Johnny Depp eventually found himself unable to meet his financial obligations. In court documents stemming from a lawsuit against his former managers, we learn Depp spent more than $2 million a month to fund his lavish lifestyle.

According to the managers' countersuit against him, Depp bought fourteen homes, totaling $75 million, paid more than $3 million a year to employ a personal staff of forty people, and spent millions on yachts. He even spent $30,000 a month on wine.[4]

# Life Hack: Keep a "Just in Case" Savings Cushion

As we discussed in Chapter 1, young Will Smith learned the hard way that enough spending can eventually empty the savings accounts of even wealthy people. Johnny Depp managed to drain a fortune dozens of times bigger than young Will Smith's, but Depp's story provides the same lesson. Always keep a "just in case" cushion in your savings account.

## Celebrity Financial Horror Story: Lindsay Lohan

### (Mismanaged Money Tool: Bills)

Actress Lindsay Lohan failed to pay her taxes (or paid only a portion of what she owed) for several years in a row. Eventually, her overdue tax bill grew to more than $230,000, and the IRS seized her bank accounts.[5]

Lohan's financial challenges actually started with mismanaging her savings. According to *Yahoo!*, the actress squandered most of her $30 million fortune on spending sprees that included millions of dollars for clothes, hotels, parties, and attorneys for her frequent legal problems.[6] And because she didn't have the money that she owed the government at tax time, Lohan failed to pay those bills—a series of missteps that could have landed her in prison.

## Life Hack: Pay Your Bills on Time—Early If Possible

Bills are a key part of your Money Toolkit because failing to pay them can lead to all sorts of financial troubles: fees, penalties, higher interest rates, lower credit scores, and even an inability to get loans. But if there's one bill you never, *ever* want to miss, it's for your taxes. That's because the entity sending you that bill—the government—has the power to put you in jail.

> **KEY TAKEAWAYS**
> - Treat the tools in your Money Toolkit with respect, and they'll help you build a successful financial life.
> - Always keep a "just in case" cushion in your savings account.
> - Pay your bills on time—and early whenever you can.

In these first two parts, we've focused exclusively on you: how *you* interact with your money, and what *you* can do to build smart financial habits. You've been the only person in the equation. But in reality, many of your financial decisions will be influenced by other people. So let's talk about that.

*Part III*

# Navigating the Social Side of Money

# 17

# *Develop a Lending Policy*

All through school, I had a friend we'll call Kenny (because that's pretty close to his real name). When we were in our early twenties, Kenny started frequently asking me to lend him money. "Robbie, can I borrow $20?" "Roberto, let me hold $50 for a minute." "Loan me $30, Big R?" *Hmm.* Now that I think about it, maybe sometimes he was actually asking other people.

Just kidding. He was always asking me. And I always said yes.

Kenny borrowed money from me dozens of times, and he never repaid a single dollar. He never even acknowledged that he owed me money when he asked to borrow more. Sometimes, when we were hanging out, he'd stop in a store and buy himself some new clothes. Clearly, Kenny and I had a very different understanding of the word "borrow." Lesson learned.

You might never face a serial borrower like Kenny, but lending money to a friend even once carries risks. It could cause you stress, you could lose the money permanently, and the loan might even damage your relationship. All because you wanted to do something nice for someone.

Let's talk about it.

## Why Do We Lend?

Most personal loans happen under one of two basic circumstances.

Circumstance one: a trusted friend asks you to borrow money. You're happy to help. So you agree to a timeframe for your friend to repay you, and you hand over the cash. Because you know this person is ethical and responsible, you're confident you'll get your money back. Doing this favor might even strengthen the friendship. You're showing kindness, and your friend gets a chance to demonstrate trustworthiness by paying you back on time. *Good experience.*

Circumstance two: someone you don't know well asks you to borrow money. You aren't close friends, so the request catches you off-guard. This person might even be counting on the fact that you won't be ready with a good reason to say no, and that's part of their strategy. (This is how Kenny operated.) You don't want to be rude or confrontational, so it's easiest just to say yes. But handing over the money to this person creates stress for you. You're not confident you'll ever see your money again. You're also wondering how long to wait before asking for it, and what you'll say when you've waited long enough. *Terrible experience.*

## Why Does It Often Go Wrong?

Obviously, you should avoid making loans under circumstance two. It's not worth the potential hassle and stress. But you should also know that even under the first circumstance, lending to someone you trust, things can go haywire. A 2024 study found that 30 percent of people who have borrowed money from friends admitted they never repaid those loans.[1]

Consider how easily two good friends could find themselves in this mess:

Friend 1: *"Hey, you owe me $20."*

Friend 2: *"No I don't."*

Friend 1: *"Remember, I lent it to you a few weeks ago when we were at the ballgame?"*

Friend 2: *"Yeah, but I paid you back when I covered your dinner after work last week."*

Friend 1: *"That wasn't paying me back. You offered to pick up the check."*

Friend 2: *"That's why I offered! Because I knew I owed you the money."*

The problem here, as you can see, is a lack of communication. Even if the borrower and lender are both acting in good faith, one person might have a different understanding of what it means to repay the loan. That's why you'll want to set up ground rules before loaning money to anyone, even close friends. We'll review some of those rules below. First, though, here's this chapter's key suggestion.

**The safest lending strategy, the one most likely to protect you from stress and damaged friendships, is not to lend money at all.**

## Have a No-Lending Policy

Personal loans cause problems in friendships all the time. In that same 2024 study, 33 percent of people said that "Repeated borrowing without repayment was a top driver of relationship tension."[2]

If you lend money to a friend who can't or won't repay it, you could develop enough resentment toward the person that you no longer want to be their friend. And here's where it gets crazy: the borrower might even start to resent *you*.

Think about it. Every time you see each other, your friend is reminded that they've taken advantage of your friendship by borrowing money from you and failing to pay you back. People don't like to feel guilty. And because your friend grows to associate that awful feeling with seeing you, some part of them becomes convinced that you're the problem.

For these reasons, it's probably best to set a universal no-lending policy.

And the best way to handle the situation when someone asks you for a loan—especially those surprise requests from people you don't know well—is to develop a standard phrase explaining why you have to say no.

## Life Hack: Create a Standard No-Lending Phrase

If someone asks you to borrow money, and you don't already have a plan to deal with this sort of request, that can be a very tense moment. Some people bumble their way through an excuse. ("I don't have enough cash on me.") But a persistent friend might try to find a way around that excuse. ("That's okay. I can wait until tomorrow, if you can get it from home.")

So develop a standard phrase for loan requests from friends. When someone asks you for a loan, you could say, "Promised my parents I wouldn't lend money. Can't go back on my word." You could also try humor. If a friend says, "Hey, I need twenty bucks," you can say, "Well, let's work together to find someone who has it." If the person keeps at it, trying new ways to ask you for the loan, you can just repeat your standard phrase.

Most people—and, I hope, all your *true* friends—will respect your position. But even those who don't will at least learn quickly that there's no point in asking you for money again.

## How to Lend Money (If You Must)

If someone you know well and trust asks you to borrow money, and you're comfortable parting with the cash for whatever time the person is asking for it, it might be okay to make the loan. But remember, these situations can lead to several problems. So you'll want to review a few ground rules upfront—first for yourself, then for your friend—and you'll want to make sure your friend acknowledges what you expect.

1. **Make sure the loan can't cause you any financial troubles**

Check with your Whole Money Picture, and make sure you can afford to be without this money for the timeframe your friend intends to borrow it.

2. **Make an explicit agreement about when and *how* your friend will pay you back**

Set a day for your friend to repay the loan and make it clear that this means bringing you the cash, making a Zelle payment into your account, or whatever terms you agree on. You don't want to get into a *But I paid for you at lunch* argument later.

3. **Let your friend know that if they're late, you'll be asking them right away**

If you don't have a plan ahead of time, asking someone for the money they owe you can be uncomfortable. One way around that challenge is to clearly state your plans to remind your friend. As you're lending them the money, you might say, "Okay, if you haven't paid me back two weeks from today, I'm going to remind you every day until you do." Then, at the two-week mark, you can just say, "Hey, it's been two weeks. This is the reminder I promised you."

### KEY TAKEAWAYS

- Develop a strategy about lending money—when to lend, when not to lend, and how to ask for repayment—so you're never caught off guard by a request.
- Set a no-lending policy for all but truly trusted friends to avoid the problems personal loans can cause.
- Always establish the rules for repaying when you do loan a friend money.

Now you've got a few tools to avoid those awkward moments when you'd rather not lend money. But what happens when you're on the other side of these situations? Next, we'll discuss when it's okay—and when it's not okay—to borrow money.

# 18

# *Be Careful Borrowing Money*

Caution: uncomfortable paragraphs ahead.

Imagine you're out shopping with friends. Everyone in your group is buying stuff. Josie got a new purse. Jordan picked up some perfume. Megan is still feeding her crazy habit for scented candles. Four new ones this time! (Can she really smell the difference between vanilla and vanilla *bean*?)

But you haven't bought anything. Not because you haven't seen stuff you'd like, but because you didn't bring any money. The reason you didn't bring any money? You don't have any. No big deal, though. You're out having fun with your friends.

Then you see an outfit you want. Really, *really* want. The problem is the outfit costs $90, which is significantly more than your $0. But you really, *really* want it. So you ask Megan to borrow the money, and she lends it to you.

Fast-forward a week. You're totally over the outfit. Old news. (You've *habituated* it.) Now something new has your attention: the looks Megan gives you when you see each other. It feels like she's upset with you. Seeing you seems to stress her out.

Also, you're not sure why, but seeing Megan is starting to stress you out, too. Why does she give you these looks? Why does she say only two or three words whenever you ask her a question? What's her problem? Is it the loan? *Good grief.* You'll pay her back. It's not like she needs the money right this minute. If she can afford to make her room smell like lavender, she can afford to go a little longer without her $90. Right?

Borrowing money from friends, at least when you can't repay them immediately, is a dangerous game. So let's talk about it.

---

**If you can't pay back a friend's loan immediately, don't ask for the money. Dragging out repaying a personal loan can damage your reputation, make you feel terrible, and even ruin your friendship.**

---

## Two Types of Borrowing from a Friend

Quick recap. In Chapter 10, we explored the two ways of using a credit card. The first way is safe: you tap, swipe, or (*Weeeee!*) wave your credit card to purchase an item, the card company loans you the money at that moment, and you pay them back in full as soon as the bill comes in. This way, you're "borrowing" only for convenience and repaying the loan right away. Using your credit card like this won't cost you anything.

Then there's the second, financially dangerous way. You use the card to buy things you can't afford, pay only a small portion of each bill, and let your outstanding balance grow month after month. This way, you're borrowing money without a plan to repay it, and that's going to cause you problems. When you engage in this unsafe credit card behavior, the financial costs are substantial: high interest charges, growing debt, and possibly late-payment penalties and even damaged credit scores.

The story is similar to borrowing from friends. There's a good way and an awful way to do it. Let's look at both scenarios: the safe one and the one you'll want to avoid like a rotten fish-scented candle.

1. **The safe scenario: you don't have the money handy**

Example: you're at lunch and realize you forgot your wallet. Your friend lends you $20. As soon as you get to your wallet, you grab $20 and bring it right to your friend. This is the safe and honorable way to borrow money.

2. **The unsafe scenario: you don't have the money, period**

Example: you borrow $90 from Megan because you really, *really* want that outfit but can't afford it yourself. Just as the financial costs of mishandling a credit card are high, you could pay a steep price in other ways for treating a friend this way. The risks of dragging out repaying your friend's loan could include an awful sense of guilt and shame, damage to your reputation, and even harm to the friendship itself.

## Life Hack: Make a Can't-Miss Reminder

If you borrow from a friend under the only honorable scenario—when you have the money but just don't have it handy—you should immediately set yourself a can't-ignore reminder that repaying this loan is your top priority. It could be a handwritten note you leave sticking out of your wallet or purse, or an email you send yourself. Make it simple. "Repay Matthew $40." That should do the trick. (Unless you borrowed from Steve.)

## Life Hack: Don't Borrow Money You Can't Repay Right Away

No loan should be worth risking your stress levels, your reputation as a good person, or the friendship of someone kind enough to loan you money in the first place. So you should never, *ever* borrow from a friend (or a credit card company, for that matter) if you're not certain you can repay the money soon.

But here's an even simpler strategy that might be easier to follow.

Don't borrow money. Don't borrow money. Don't borrow money. Don't borrow money. Go ahead and borrow money. (*Just checking.*) Don't borrow money. Don't borrow money. Don't borrow money.

Okay, let's hope that worked.

---

**KEY TAKEAWAYS**

- Don't borrow money you can't repay immediately.
- Failing to promptly repay a loan from a friend can cause stress for both your friend and you, and it can even wreck the friendship.
- As soon as you borrow from a friend, write yourself a can't-miss-it note (like an email to yourself) so you remember to pay it back right away.

---

We just talked about the serious risks of borrowing to pay for something *you* want. But what happens when what's driving you to buy isn't you at all, but *other people*? Let's talk about how to avoid spending out of peer pressure.

# 19

# *Watch Out for Peer Pressure*

Here's the scenario. Your friends are really excited about an upcoming event: a concert, a big game, everyone's favorite stand-up comedian coming to your city, whatever. Your buddies are all buying tickets—which cost a fortune—and they're asking you to buy one, too. In fact, they're not just asking. Even though you've told them you're trying to save money and really can't afford a ticket, they're still begging, nagging, even demanding that you go with them. This is a *Friends Night Out*, they insist, and you're part of the group.

So here's the question. Which is the more ethical decision: buying the ticket to support your friends' enthusiasm for the event, or disappointing them because you need to save?

That was a trick question. Real friends wouldn't pressure you this way. They'd never want you to undermine your financial goals just so they could have a little more fun on their big night out. There's no ethical dilemma here at all. Save your money. And if necessary, find better friends.

> If you have friends who pressure you to spend money when you can't or don't want to, you need better friends.

## Peer Pressure Should Be Positive, or It Should Be Resisted

Peer pressure can be a powerful driver of behavior, especially for young people. There's a reason parents say to their kids, "If your friends were jumping off a cliff, would you jump, too?" It's not because you're likely to make *better* decisions when you're surrounded by your peer group. One huge meta-study on the effects of peer pressure found that adolescents' driving was 50 percent riskier when they were with their peers. Examining crime statistics, that same study found young people typically commit delinquent acts in peer groups, not alone.[1] And getting back to our topic—spending money—here's a finding from research published by the US Department of Education: "In contrast to parents' positive influence, peers tend to stimulate less responsible spending behaviors by encouraging materialism and by recommending purchases."[2]

Now you can see why parents around the world are always asking that cliff-jumping question. When they catch their kid doing something stupid, the kid often responds by saying, "But Jeremy did it." (Honestly, sometimes I wish this Jeremy character *would* jump off a cliff.)

We're discussing peer pressure only in terms of its negative consequences. But there's also a positive form of peer pressure. True friends, the quality people you want in your life, will lift you up. They'll pressure you to be the best version of yourself: to study when you're feeling lazy, to step back from the cliff and stop acting like an idiot, and to save your money if they know you're running low. More of that peer pressure, please! You've just got to watch out for the other type of peer pressure—the pressure to spend (or drive) more recklessly.

Am I suggesting that any friend who pushes you to buy things, or gives you a hard time when you don't, is trying to undermine you? Not at all. In fact, they're probably affected by the same hidden emotional drivers we talked about in Part I. Your friends could be under the spell of advertisers' messages. They might have fallen into the dangerous habit of buying things out of boredom or because their brain is craving endorphins or dopamine. To validate their own spending, they might want you to make the same types of purchases they're making. Without even knowing it, your friends could be subconsciously hoping that by influencing your spending behaviors, they'll feel better about the decisions they're making, because some part of their brain knows those decisions are foolish.

Just remember that as of 2024, the average young person has racked up thousands of dollars in credit card debt.[3] Unless you know your friends are responsible with money and have a smart financial plan, you probably don't want to rely on them for spending advice.

## Life Hack: Have a Standard Phrase

Just as you'll want a go-to phrase to avoid being caught off guard by someone asking to borrow money, you can also create a standard phrase for the times your friends want you to spend, but you'd rather not. It can be as simple as, "I'm watching my money for a while." That should end the debate—assuming you're dealing with a real friend.

You can also offer a little more explanation with your standard phrase: "I'm trying a new approach to money, spending only when I really want something. It's working out well so far. I'm saving a lot and buying a lot less junk." That answer might open up some debate, but maybe you'd prefer that. It could even get your friends interested in hearing more about your new philosophy, which could give you a chance to share with them what you've learned about being a money savvy teen.

## Life Hack: Choose Your Peers Wisely

Let's work the problem from the other angle. Rather than learning tips and tricks for handling difficult peer pressure situations, a better strategy might be to insist on friends who wouldn't put you in those dilemmas in the first place.

If you're feeling peer pressure to spend money you don't have, or to do or buy things you'd rather not, then these peers probably aren't true friends anyway. And you deserve better.

> ### KEY TAKEAWAYS
>
> - If you feel uneasy about a purchase your friends want you to make, remember that most young people are in debt. Go with your instincts and save your cash.
> - Develop a go-to phrase when your peers pressure you to spend money. It could be as simple as "I'm watching my money for a while."
> - Choose your peers wisely—and the only type of peer pressure you'll feel is the good kind, the kind that pushes you to be a better version of yourself.

Now you have a few tools to hang onto your cash when your peers want to pressure you to part with it. But what about those times you do want to part with your money—specifically, to donate it to causes you care about? In the next chapter, we'll talk about developing a Giving Plan.

# 20

# *Create a Giving Plan*

Let me start with a confession. When I was in my twenties, I made an idiotic mistake. (Okay, lots of them, but only one I'm willing to share here.) Not long after I bought my first condo, someone called me at home, claiming to represent a charity that "supports our local fire department" or something. The man was convincing. The firefighters were apparently counting on my help so they could afford things like extra equipment to stay safe in the field. I couldn't let these heroes down, so I donated $100, and I felt great about it.

But then, almost immediately, the same guy called again. And then again. And again.

I started looking into this so-called charity and found some disturbing articles about it—and other ones like it. Turns out some dishonest people have found loopholes in the law that let them set up "nonprofit organizations," collect donations they promise will support some cause, and distribute only a small percentage of that money to their supposed mission. Where does the rest go? Who knows? (*Champagne in the conference room, everybody!*)

I don't want you to assume the typical charitable organization is a scam. Far from it. Most are ethical, devoted to their cause, and work hard to keep their expenses low so they can steer as much money as possible to the people they're trying to help. But here's what I am saying: don't be an idiot like I was. If you want to donate a portion of your money to causes you care about, you need to be strategic about it. Create a giving plan.

---

Develop a plan for when, how, and to which causes you'll donate money. For every fundraising request that falls outside this plan, prepare a few standard phrases explaining why you can't donate.

---

## Three Questions for Any Donation Request

The world has finite resources. Life is a struggle for many people. As you get older, you'll encounter donation requests for all types of causes. People will knock on your door collecting money for a group helping children. The person checking out your groceries at the supermarket will ask if you'd like to support the local school fundraiser. Coworkers will ask you to give money to help fight some disease. Videos on YouTube will show heartbreaking images of starving people, injured animals, or towns devastated by natural disasters—and ask you to make a generous donation.

I'm all in favor of giving. One of the best things you can do with your wealth is use it to help others. In fact, you'll also discover there's a selfish reason to make charitable contributions: it feels great. But you need to keep a few things in mind about giving.

1. **Do you have money to spare?**

Charitable giving can represent a higher purpose than buying a new pair of shoes, but donating money is still a form of spending. That means you need to place it in the context of your Whole Money

Picture. Ask yourself: *can I really afford to give this money now? Will doing so hurt Monday Me?*

**2. Is the organization legit?**

Most nonprofits and charitable organizations do great work. But you can't just click the donate link every time you see a video showing an adorable animal suffering. You should also be careful about people collecting for charity in unusual places, like a parking lot or over the phone. Before you commit any of your money, you need to research those asking for it, to make sure their organization is real. (More on that below.)

**3. What's your giving strategy?**

People and organizations will approach you often for donations. If you don't have a strategy for when to donate (and when not to), you could find yourself giving away money in situation after situation because you didn't feel comfortable saying no. Like my serial borrower friend Kenny, some people fundraising for charity count on this and try to catch you off guard. Without a giving plan, you could donate for the wrong reasons to causes you don't value—and be left without enough money to support the causes that matter to you.

## Ideas for a Smart Giving Plan

Time to get proactive about your charitable donations. The easiest way to build a strategic giving plan is to ask yourself some basic questions. For example:

- *What types of causes do I want to support?*
- *Is there a dollar amount, or a percentage of my income, that I want to donate?*

- *Should I distribute my charitable contributions throughout the year or hold most of my "donation budget" them until the end-of-year holidays?*

You'll think of other questions that matter to you. When you're done, your answers should represent a good policy for giving. It might look like this:

*I plan to donate $300 a year to charity, and I will give only to one of three causes: needy families, cancer research, and helping the American Red Cross.*

Or this:

*I plan to donate 5 percent of my income, and I will reserve it all for the end of the year, so I can donate to charities that help the poor and hungry during the holidays.*

## Life Hack: Check with Charity Watchdogs

As part of your strategic giving plan, you should always do a little research on any charitable organization before handing them your money. Check with sites like GiveWell.org and CharityWatch.org to see what they say about the charity asking for your donation.

## Life Hack: Have a Standard Phrase

Just as you'll want a standard phrase to politely turn down the would-be borrower who tries to catch you off guard (*Sorry, promised my parents I wouldn't loan money*), you'll also want some standard phrases ready for the would-be fundraiser who surprises you with a donation request. A few examples:

- *I give only to certain charities.*
- *I've donated all the money I can spare this year.*
- *Sorry, but I'm broke.*

## Life Hack: Add Donations to Your Budget

To make sure your generosity doesn't undermine your Whole Money Picture, you'll want to track your donations in your budget. You could include them on your list of variable expenses if you expect to give different amounts at different times, or you can add them as a fixed expense if you'll be giving the same amount to the same charities each month or year.

> **KEY TAKEAWAYS**
>
> - Create a plan to decide when, how, and to which causes you'll donate money.
> - Have a standard phrase ready for donation requests that don't align with your giving plan. That way, you won't be caught off guard.
> - Always check the track records of charities before donating. You can use rating sites like GiveWell.org and CharityWatch.org

Okay, we've discussed how to channel your generous nature to make sure you donate your money safely, effectively, and according to both your charitable goals and your budget. But what about your less-charitable impulses? In the next chapter, we'll discuss the downsides of treating money as a competition.

# 21

# *Remind Yourself that Money Isn't a Competition*

If I hadn't double-checked the following statistics to make sure they came from credible sources, I would've assumed somebody made them up. According to a major study, more than a third of all home improvement projects happen only because the homeowner wants to impress or outdo friends or neighbors. In fact, the average homeowner spends more than $3,500 on these projects—all because they're feeling competitive about other people's houses.[1]

Don't get me wrong. I'm a huge fan of home improvements. Your home will be one of the largest and most important purchases you'll ever make. You'll probably spend as much time there as you do in any other environment. There are plenty of legitimate reasons to invest in renovating or upgrading the place you live. But *My kitchen needs to be better than Theo's!* isn't one of them. Imagine trying to defend such a costly home project—redoing your whole kitchen—just because someone you know upgraded theirs.

### Scene: The (Perfectly Nice) Kitchen of Hayden and Taylor

Hayden: *Taylor, did you notice at the party last night that Theo remodeled his kitchen? That thing looks amazing.*

Taylor: *I like our kitchen.*

Hayden: *Yeah, I did, too. But it's time to up our game. Besides, what makes Theo think he's better than we are?*

Taylor: *I know Theo didn't say that.*

Hayden: *He didn't have to say it. His new kitchen says it for him. We should do an even bigger upgrade here.*

Taylor: *Hayden, that'll cost a fortune.*

Hayden: *We have the money in savings. Well, most of it. Let's build the sleekest, most gorgeous kitchen in the neighborhood. Imagine the look on Theo's face when he sees it.*

Taylor: *Okay, what's happening here, Hayden? Do you want a better kitchen? Or do you want to see a look on Theo's face?*

Hayden: *Don't forget Andre and Jasmine. They have such a great sense of design. Think about how impressed they'll be.*

Taylor: *I have an idea. Instead of going into debt just so we can demolish this perfectly nice kitchen and build a more expensive one, how about we just pay all these people to come over, look at our kitchen, and make "impressed" faces?*

If only everyone could be as sensible as Taylor.

---

**When you spend to outdo (or keep up with) friends, you're buying things not because you want them but because you want to prove to other people you can afford those things. What's the point in that?**

---

## The Dangers of Social Comparison

We live in the wealthiest time in human history. By almost every measure (health, lifespan, income, leisure time, entertainment, etc.), you're going to enjoy a standard of living that's better than even the world's richest people just a few centuries ago could've imagined. So why do so many people today, even affluent people, seem so unhappy?

One of the big culprits is social comparison, which is more prevalent than ever thanks to social media. For most of our history, humans lived among small traveling tribes and then, more recently, permanent villages and eventually cities. Throughout that history, we spent most of our lives surrounded by people who lived the way we did, with roughly the same material possessions and living standards that we had. Few nomads suffered anxiety from noticing that *Sven's satchels are always fancier than mine*.

Your generation faces a challenge that's brand-new to humankind. Reviewing the dark side of social media, Dan Bates, PhD, writes in *Psychology Today* that "When we consistently view carefully curated snapshots of our peers' successes, exotic vacations, or picture-perfect relationships, it's easy to fall into the trap of believing that our own lives are lacking in comparison."[2]

The frustrating irony is that as civilization's overall prosperity increases, lifting most people's living standards up with it, modern communications and technologies make it easier than ever to observe people *living even better* than we are. That can trigger the unhealthy feeling of competitiveness that drains Hayden and Taylor's savings account, just so they can build a kitchen they don't need.

## You're a Hopeless Romantic

There's another reason many people feel competitive about money. And unlike social media, this one did affect our ancestors. Dr. Raj Patel, the pediatrician we met in Chapter 1, told me that when we spend to show off or to one-up our peers, we're engaging in an age-old behavior that's common to most forms of life.

"The impulse to spend money competitively is often humans' way of trying to attract a mate," Dr. Patel said. "Animals of all types engage in this type of competition. A bird will spend hours cleaning its environment to make the space more appealing for a mate. It's their equivalent of furnishing and decorating their apartment to impress a date."

Unlike birds, we have cash and credit cards. So our rituals look a bit different. But as Dr. Patel explained, we're essentially doing the same thing. "We spend money grooming ourselves and buying nice houses, cars, clothes—all, on some level, for the evolutionary goal of reproducing our genes. If Daryn has a nicer car than we do, we might get a nagging feeling that we need a better car because if we don't, Daryn might drive off with our potential mate."

Fortunately, we're not birds. If we want to attract a mate, we can use our words. And now that you understand what drives a lot of humans' competitive impulses about spending money—unnecessary social comparisons and the goal of reproducing—you should be able to avoid a lot of the sillier decisions you'll see your peers making.

## Spending to Keep Up with Peers Is Just as Crazy

I hope you see the lunacy and the completely wasted effort and money of spending on flashy things just to impress or outdo other people.

But what if the situation is reversed? What if your peers are spending lots of money, making you feel like you need to do the same just to keep up? Let me show you why that behavior is just as ridiculous. And grab the popcorn, because I'm going to illustrate my point with some crazy stories.

When the Federal Reserve Bank of Philadelphia studied the effects of income differences among peers, their research uncovered an amazing phenomenon. When people win the lottery, their *neighbors* are more likely to go bankrupt soon afterward. Here's the study's key insight: "We find that the magnitude of the neighbor's lottery win is related to the dollar value of *more visible* but not less visible consumption assets of neighboring bankruptcy filers."[3] In other words, the more lotto money their neighbors win, the more money people feel compelled to spend on big, flashy purchases the whole neighborhood can see—like expensive cars and costly upgrades to the exterior of the home. Unfortunately, as the research found, trying to keep up with their lottery-winning neighbors can lead people to spend themselves into bankruptcy.

If you think spending to keep up is just a bizarre quirk of average income earners whose neighbors hit a jackpot, consider this. According to research, 78 percent of professional athletes go broke within three years after retiring.[4] How could people who earn millions of dollars find themselves with nothing when their careers end? One reason, former NBA player Erick Strickland told *Sports Illustrated*, is the pressure to keep up with your new social circle. "For rookies, it's like an unspoken initiation. You're trying to get in good with the veterans, so you go beyond your means. You drive the nice car, splurge on the nice house."[5]

Here's one more crazy story, one involving my old boss. I was working for a startup whose CEO had recently earned millions of dollars after cashing out of his previous company. He was a friendly guy, but most days he seemed anxious, even miserable. Then one day a vice president at the company, a close friend of the CEO, told me the reason for his stress. *He's got a few million,* she explained. *But after his first company made money, he joined the rich crowd. Among his new peer group, he has the least money. He needs another big score just to keep up with them.*

I trust you're seeing the pattern. No matter how much money you make, you can always find people nearby who have even more. Spending to keep up with them can cause you stress, drain your savings, and even send you into bankruptcy. And it almost certainly won't make you happier.

## A Game with No Winners

If spending money to keep up with peers can create problems even for a wealthy entrepreneur who has enough money to retire, imagine how much financial damage this behavior can cause the average person who doesn't have a lot of extra cash. Rather than enjoying the money they earn, they waste it trying to create the appearance that they have more than they do.

This game has no winners. Even if you manage to spend enough to keep up with all your friends, what have you won? You'll have spent yourself into financial trouble just so that you could demonstrate (falsely) that you can afford expensive things. But those people won't be impressed anyway, because they can afford those things, too.

And if someone in your social circle starts buying new things that no one else in the group has yet, what then? If you want to keep up, you'll have to go out and buy more stuff. It never ends.

## With Friends Like These

Chances are, if you're spending to keep up with real friends, the pressure you're feeling is only in your head. If you wore different clothes or suggested less expensive places to eat, your friends would understand. If you have true friends, which I'll assume you do, the last thing they'd want is for you to go broke trying to impress them.

On the other hand, if any of your friends *would* think less of you because you don't have as much money as they have, who needs them? You deserve better people in your life than that. The problem corrects itself.

And by the way, how do you even know your friends can afford the things they're buying? The saddest irony would be spending money you don't have just to keep up with peers who are buying stuff *they* can't afford because they want to show off to you.

## Life Hack: Be Honest About What You Can and Can't Afford

Your best strategy is to be completely honest with your friends. If you can't afford something they're buying or doing, tell them. You'll have a lot less stress not trying to keep up with everyone in your group. And you'll have a lot more money.

My parents have a great story about this. Their closest friends, another married couple, suggested a big vacation overseas. My parents were interested but said they didn't want to spend a lot of money on the trip. And because their friends liked to travel expensively, my parents recommended that the couple should just go on this vacation themselves. But instead, their friends responded this way: *Let's make a game out of it. Tell us how much you want to spend, and we'll use that as our budget. Then we'll hunt for hotels, restaurants, and tours that will keep us under that budget. It'll be fun.*

Those are the types of friends you want.

## Life Hack: Picture the Royals' Bathroom Routine

As I noted above, you were born into a better standard of living than almost anyone in history has ever been able to enjoy. So here's a counterintuitive life hack. One great way to counteract the downsides of social comparison is to compare yourself to *more* people, people around the world and throughout history, not just your friends or some social media influencer with a mansion.

Take a wider-angle view of the human story and you'll discover that in comparison to us, almost all our ancestors lived very difficult lives—even the richest people of their times. If you have a strong stomach, you might want to learn about the horrifying hygienic practices even wealthy families had to engage in until very recently. Whenever you feel like your life doesn't measure up because of Daryn's car or whatever, just picture a king marching out of his palace in the middle of the night, trudging through the mud to reach the royal garden, so he can go to the bathroom. That's right: for most of history, even a nation's number one had to go outside to do number two.

Speaking of which, let's end this chapter with a fun fact. One of the inventors credited with bringing us the indoor flush toilet is a man named Thomas Crapper. (Don't believe me? Look it up.)

> **KEY TAKEAWAYS**
>
> - Avoid social comparison. You can easily find people who have more than you do, but so what? The question is whether you're happy with what you have.
> - Remember that a lot of competitiveness about money stems from a biological need to reproduce. If you've got some game, you don't need expensive shoes.
> - Be honest with your peers about what you can and can't afford. If they're real friends, they would never want you to go broke pretending.

You might have noticed that we're moving into the darker corners of human nature: feeling competitive about money, spending more than you can afford just to create appearances for your more affluent peers. These are not humans' most admirable qualities.

And if you're game, I'd like to go a little farther down this path. But bring your flashlight, because it's about to get even darker. Next, we'll discuss feeling jealous about other people's money.

# 22

# *Slay the Green-Eyed Monster*

There's a funny old fable about two brothers, Boris and Ivan. Both men have the same amount of wealth and almost identical material possessions. But there's one difference: Boris has a goat, and Ivan doesn't. One day, Ivan encounters a genie, who offers to grant him any wish he'd like. The genie recommends that he should think carefully about his decision, because he has only one wish. Ignoring the suggestion, Ivan responds immediately: "I want Boris's goat to die."

Jealousy is among our darker traits, and most of us don't like to admit we feel it. But it's part of human nature, especially when it comes to wealth. A recent study found that nearly three in five adults (57 percent) have felt envious of someone else's financial situation.[1] (And if you ask me, this means that the study also accidentally found that 43 percent of adults are liars.)

With endless opportunities to engage in social comparison today, thanks to the internet and social media, you might find yourself facing this perfectly natural emotion at any time. So it's a good idea to learn some strategies that can help you counteract the nasty effects of money jealousy. One strategy when you're feeling jealous: just ask yourself a few questions.

1. **Do I know they're happier than I am?**

You've seen the news stories. Celebrities and other high-profile rich people overdose on drugs, get themselves into trouble with the law, and even commit suicide. One antidote to feeling jealous of someone else's wealth is to think about what those sad stories mean. No amount of money (or fame or power or beauty or *anything*) will necessarily make a person happier. In fact, as these common stories suggest, more money can even make people unhappy. Why feel jealous toward someone who might well be less happy than you are?

2. **Do I know even if they're truly better off financially than I am?**

Remember, the average American adult in 2024 was more than $6,300 in credit card debt.[2] Some of those big, expensive things your friends are buying—the purchases that trigger your jealousy—aren't always indications that they have more money than you do. They might even be clues that the opposite is true: your friends are spending themselves into a financial hole, while you—the money savvy teen that you are—are keeping your money safe and growing.

3. **Is feeling this way affecting my well-being?**

According to the study I cited above, 54 percent of Americans said money envy negatively impacts their mental health. In fact, the number was higher for younger generations than it was for older people.[3] If you start feeling jealous about what someone else has, try to remind yourself that the feeling itself accomplishes nothing (you can't *be jealous* your way to anything positive) and that it could even cause other negative outcomes like anxiety and depression.

One way to avoid jealousy over other people's money is to do a little research. The biggest studies into money and happiness find that above a modest income, people don't become happier with more money.

## Life Hack: Save Boris's Goat!

Poor Ivan isn't jealous of Boris's goat itself. If he were, he'd ask the genie to give the goat to him, not to kill it. He feels jealous of what he imagines is his brother's better life, which the goat symbolizes, and he wishes to take that away from Boris.

Unfortunately, in addition to a broken moral compass, Ivan is also lacking in logic. The fact that someone has a bigger bank account, or a higher-paying job, tells us nothing about whether that person has a better life than we do. There's scientific evidence that after acquiring a certain number of goats, almost nobody gets any happier. Two Nobel Prize-winning economists who studied this question over several decades have come to the following conclusion: "Beyond $75,000 in the contemporary United States, however, higher income is neither the road to experience happiness nor the road to relief of unhappiness or stress"[4]

Instead of devoting any energy to jealousy over other people's money, be grateful for what you have—and celebrate their success as well. You'll feel better.

Sorry, Ivan. You wasted your wish.

## Life Hack: Don't Count Other People's Money

Jealousy can also show up disguised as something else: *counting* other people's money. You might tell yourself that you're not jealous, just curious about what other people have or how much they earn. Just doing your research, that's all, learning a few facts about your colleagues or friends. But this, unfortunately, is just jealousy dressed in nicer clothes.

You'll almost certainly encounter people like this in your career. They'll want to know what their coworkers are earning. They'll complain often about how much the company pays its executives. And they'll always be on the lookout for some new hire who's somehow getting paid more than they are.

Don't be one of those people.

> ### KEY TAKEAWAYS
>
> - Jealousy is a universal human trait, so don't feel ashamed for experiencing it. But it can undermine your well-being, so you do need to fight against it.
> - The research shows that more money doesn't mean more happiness. Why waste time feeling jealous of someone who might be less happy than you are?
> - Remember that the average adult is in debt. Your friends' flashy purchases shouldn't trigger your jealousy; they should trigger your sympathy.

Tough chapter, right? We talked about unhappiness, celebrity downfalls, drug overdoses, even goat killing. That's jealousy for you—a very dark aspect of the human condition.

And if you're willing to go just a little farther down this path, we've got a few more dark traits to explore. But first, let me caution you against a social practice that's often completely innocent but can cause lots of problems in relationships: telling people how much money you have.

# 23

# *Keep the Details of Your Money Situation to Yourself*

Apple or Android. Dodgers or Yankees. Coke or Pepsi. Marvel or DC. Cheese or pepperoni. Some topics seem almost designed to spike blood pressure and start huge arguments. Thankfully, most friendships can survive heated debates over topics like these. But there is one that can really put a relationship at risk: money. Specifically, talking about how much you have or earn.

## What's Your Social Security Number?

Other than immediate family, I strongly advise you not to talk with anybody about what you make or how much you have in the bank. Here's a good rule of thumb: if you'd feel strange telling the person your Social Security Number (or asking for theirs), don't give them the details of your financial situation. I also strongly suggest not asking people how much money *they* make or have. There are no good reasons to share this information with almost anybody in your life, and there are lots of reasons to avoid doing so. Here are some of the big ones.

1. **You could become resentful of the other person**

   Friend 1: *I have $12,391 in my savings account. How about you?*
   Friend 2: *Let me check my banking app.* [Hits buttons on phone.] *Whoa. You're not going to believe this. I have $12,391 too. That's amazing!*

Yeah, that would be amazing. It's also the only circumstance where neither friend would have reason to feel uncomfortable, guilty, or resentful. And because it's never going to happen, conversations like this will almost always end with one of the friends feeling bad in some way.

Imagine you blurt out *I have $12,391 in my savings account. How about you?* Now imagine your friend says, *About $75,000.* Are you going to be able to look at your friend again without feeling resentful or wondering how they got their hands on so much money?

2. **The other person could become resentful of you.**

See above.

3. **Discovering you earn more might make you feel guilty.**

Let's say you tell a friend your salary, just in the spirit of sharing information. Your friend responds by sharing their details. It turns out you make a lot more money, and now you both know it. After that conversation, you notice your friend behaving less confidently and positively around you. You're concerned that you've made this person feel less worthy or even inadequate, and you could be right.

4. **The other person could think you're bragging.**

If you tell a friend your income or the size of your bank account, and it's more than they have, your friend might think you said it to show off. Even if your motives were innocent, even if you were sharing only because you thought it would bring you and your friend closer, the conversation could backfire and leave your friend thinking you're someone who needs to feel superior. This is especially true if you have more money than your friend (even if you had no idea which one of you had more when you shared your financial details).

5. **The other person could start expecting your generosity.**

Let's say you tell some friends what you make, and it turns out your salary is the highest in the group. What if some of these friends start asking you to pay for everyone's movie tickets or for gas money every time you all go out? It might seem unfair to you—and it might be unfair—but you did give them all a reason to think you can afford more than they can. You'll have only yourself to blame.

---

**Sharing personal details about money can create problems in relationships. It's better to have a policy of not discussing these things.**

---

## Life Hack: Don't Share Specific Numbers

Let's say you get a raise at work. Am I suggesting you shouldn't tell even your closest friends about your good news? Not at all. Tell them. Celebrate with them. (And if you can afford it, pick up the check at your celebratory dinner.) Just don't discuss the dollar amount. It's fine to share that you got a five percent raise. It's not fine to tell everybody how much money that actually means.

## Life Hack: Have a Standard Phrase

Now you know not to go blurting your own money details to friends. But what if a friend asks you? Like an unexpected request to borrow money, a question like this can put you in a tricky spot. You don't want to get specific about what you have, but you don't want to be rude. What should you do?

Just as we discussed in the chapter on lending, I'd recommend preparing a standard phrase for this type of situation. Even if the question comes as a total surprise, you'll be ready with something like, "I never talk about money." Easy.

## Life Hack: Choose Your Preferences Wisely

Okay, this final life hack isn't directly related to our discussion about not telling people what you earn, but I thought it was important to guide you toward some important life decisions. So here are the correct answers from above: Apple, Dodgers, Coke (obviously), Marvel, and cheese (although in a pinch, pepperoni is an acceptable backup).

---

### KEY TAKEAWAYS

- Telling people what you earn (and asking them what they earn) can cause friction in relationships. Don't do it.

- Feel free to talk with trusted friends about financial wins (*I got a raise!*) and losses (*my investments are getting crushed!*). Just avoid sharing specifics.

- Prepare a standard phrase for shutting down these conversations before they can become awkward. "I never talk about money" should do the trick.

Just a few chapters to go. And as I warned earlier, for some of these final thoughts, we're going dark again. In our next chapter, we'll discuss the financial behavior that makes me angrier than any other: trying to mislead people into thinking you have more money than you do.

# 24

# *Don't Pretend You Have More Than You Do*

I've been putting off adding this story to the book, partly because the story itself makes me sad and partly because this concept in general—pretending you have more money than you do—makes my blood boil. But it's important you hear the awful places this dark compulsion can lead, so you'll know not to start down the path. Besides, we're in the book's final chapters, and I'm running out of room to stall. So let's just get it over with.

A friend of mine from childhood went on to become a highly successful semi-public figure. (We'll leave it at that.) He ran with a lot of celebrities. I assume he felt intimidated by the tremendous wealth he saw among his colleagues, the way my old boss did when he joined *the rich crowd* and realized he had less money than anyone else in that group. So my friend displayed all the common traits of someone constantly trying to demonstrate his wealth and status. He talked about money all the time. He posted those annoying (but mostly sad) social media pictures showing off his lavish vacations and expensive cars. (*#GoodLife!*) And he'd find a way to work the fact that he was rich and powerful into every discussion and social media post.

After spending himself down to the bottom of his bank account, my friend still felt the need to keep up appearances for his wealthy social circle. His alleged crimes started with writing bad checks, defrauding businesses out of hundreds of thousands of dollars. That led to arrests and prosecutions. Then, according to police reports, my friend escalated to burglary, grand theft, and I can't keep writing about this, so that's the end of the story.

Imagine working hard, succeeding in your profession, becoming rich—and then throwing it all away because you felt the need to pretend you were even richer. Of all the foolish financial behaviors we've discussed in this book, I can't think of one that's dumber than spending yourself into debt (or even jail) just to give other people the false impression that you have money.

So now I'm going to go all Dad on you. Sorry in advance.

---

**The surest way to avoid feeling the need to pretend you have more money than you do is to surround yourself with high-quality friends. These people don't care how much you have anyway.**

---

## Congrats. You Fooled Them. Now What?

Let's say your constant spending on flashy items has its intended effect. Your social circle becomes convinced you're rich. Super successful. Big baller. What happens then? I can't think of a single positive thing that can come from this deception. But here are a few bad outcomes I can imagine.

1. **Your friends think you have money, and they want some**

Careful what you wish for. As they see you throw around cash on clothes, electronics, maybe a fancy car (none of which you can really afford), some of your friends might come to you asking for loans or even expecting you to pay for every outing. Still glad you fooled them?

2. **Your friends overspend to keep up with *you***

We've discussed how easy it can be for someone to feel pressured by their peer group to spend more than they can afford. In this scenario, it'll be you applying that pressure. Think of how sad (and silly) it will be if you spend to make your friends think you have more than you do—and then some of them do the same, putting themselves into debt just to keep up with *you*. Some friend you are.

3. **You spend all your money, and then some**

You spend big, buy the latest and most expensive *everything*, and now everybody thinks you're rich. You weren't rich to begin with, but now the situation is far worse. You're broke. All you have to show for your big deception is a pile of Tomorrow's Junk. Oh, and probably some credit card debt. Great plan, wasn't it?

4. **You impress a bunch of shallow, superficial "friends"**

What was the point of this whole game? To show off to the type of people who judge their friends by how much money they have? Well, congratulations. Now a bunch of those shallow people think you're okay. I hope you enjoy hanging out with them, talking about some celebrity's jewelry, the latest designer shoes, and blah, blah, blah. Sounds like a lot of fun.

## Life Hack: Find Friends You'll Never Need to Impress

I know I'm repeating myself here (*sorry—still in Dad mode*), but this is really important. Instead of spending money because you hope it'll win the attention of a group of status-obsessed, shallow people, just find higher-caliber friends.

## Life Hack: Don't Spend to Create Illusions

When it comes to spending your money (as with most things in life), your best bet is just to be yourself. Never buy things to impress other people. Spend your money only on things that improve the quality of your life.

If you can stick to that rule, you'll find yourself spending a lot less than your peers do. And that's how people build real wealth. As Certified Public Accountant Jerry Markell summed it up for me, "Having money does not mean you need to spend it." Preach on, brother.

> **KEY TAKEAWAYS**
> 
> - If you feel pressure to act like you have more money than you do, you might need to re-evaluate your social group. True friends won't judge you that way.
> - Another danger of spending like you have big money is that your real friends might overspend to keep up with *you*. Don't put them in that position.
> - The simplest strategy is just to be yourself. Buy things only if they'll add value to your life—and never because you want to impress people.

You're almost done. But in these last couple of chapters, we'll still be covering some dark territory. Next up: the dangers of expecting other people's money.

# 25

# *Remember That Other People's Money Is Other People's Money*

Great news: your grandfather just won a multimillion-dollar lottery. Congratulations. Your family is going over to his house to celebrate. So, what are you thinking right now? Be honest. Actually, you don't have to tell me; I already know. *How much is he going to give me?*

Oh, and here's some bad news. An elderly cousin just died. Condolences. Your family is going to your aunt's house to discuss the arrangements. What are you thinking now? I already know. *I wonder if she left me anything.*

It's human nature to think about what our friends and relatives have, especially if they have more than we do. But there's a big, bright ethical line between noticing the wealth someone else has and feeling that *we're entitled* to some of it. We aren't.

---

**Everyone handles money differently. Some people are financially generous; others aren't. Don't assume a rich friend or family member feels an obligation to share their money with you.**

---

## More Money, More Problems

People with money face different challenges from the rest of us, but they do face challenges. One common rich-person problem is figuring out how to deal with frequent money requests or even demands from friends and family. Agreeing to every loan and saying yes to every relative's request to fund a new business venture could quickly erode their fortune. However, if these rich folks turn down every request for money, some of the people in their lives might come to resent or even hate them.

I'm not suggesting you should feel sorry for a wealthy family member or friend. I just want you to keep in mind that money can create difficulties for all of us, even rich people. If you behave like you're entitled to some of a wealthy relative's cash, you'll become one of those difficulties.

But if you still believe Uncle Barry *owes* you a new car just because he has money in the bank, let me give you a few reasons that he might disagree.

## You're Buying Me Only One Car?

**1. You might not be the first (or even the tenth) person to ask**

You might think of Uncle Barry as "rich," but that word can mean a lot of different things. Unless he's one of those people who tells you exactly how much he has and where he spends his money (something rich people rarely do), you don't know the full story of his financial situation.

What if he's paying rent, mortgage, college tuition, or other bills to support struggling family members? He'd probably never tell you about it, because those are your relatives as well, and he wouldn't want to embarrass them in front of the family.

And what if he hasn't developed a standard no-lending phrase—so he's constantly handing over money to every brazen friend who pops out of the bushes to request some cash?

If he's already dealing with these obligations, do you think your uncle wants to hear from yet another relative asking for some of his money?

### 2. This person might not be as rich as you think

Let's say Uncle Barry has been retired and "rich" (according to your family) for years, and let's say in all that time, he's never given you any money or bought you any expensive gifts. Is that because he's selfish, cheap, or uncaring? Or is it because he can't afford all the things you assume he can.

If he buys you a car, and one for your sister, and ones for each of your cousins, that might be it for Uncle Barry's retirement account.

### 3. Your relative might not want to set an unrepeatable precedent

Even if your uncle can afford to buy new cars now for each of his nephews and nieces, what happens later? As each relative's next birthday comes up, does he have to buy them all something extravagant and expensive again? He did buy everyone a car, after all, and maybe now they'll all expect equally costly gifts for every occasion. If his next birthday presents are new shirts or small-dollar Starbucks gift cards, will these relatives be disappointed? Angry? Are they already expecting him to buy each of them their *next* new car as well?

Besides, your uncle might have other ways of showing generosity. Maybe he's always there when you need him and gives his time freely to people who ask for it. That's a legitimate gift as well—and probably a better one than anything with a price tag.

4. **This rich relative might have had bad experiences giving family money**

Maybe when Uncle Barry became rich for the first time, he freely gave away money and gifts to people he cared about. And maybe some of those people came right back to him asking for more—and showing resentment when he said no.

Your rich uncle might avoid giving you money not because he doesn't care about you but because he *does* care about you. If he's seen firsthand how a rich relative's gifts can create problems for the recipient—like entitlement, greed, and a lack of ambition—your uncle might believe he's doing you a favor by not sending you down that path too. And he's probably right.

Thanks, Uncle Barry!

## Life Hack: Imagine the Roles Reversed

One way not to fall into the trap of expecting other people's money is to imagine yourself on the other side of the table. You don't need to be rich in this hypothetical, just someone with a little more in the bank than your friends have. Now imagine one of those friends saying you should pick up the tab every time you go out, or that they shouldn't have to repay the cash they borrowed from you the other day—because you "have money."

Not a good feeling, is it? You're responsible for your money. Your friends are responsible for theirs. And that's my point.

## KEY TAKEAWAYS

- It's okay to notice that someone in your life has money. In fact, it's human nature. But it's not okay to assume you're entitled to any of that money.
- People with money might have legitimate reasons not to give it to friends and family—and some of their reasons might be to protect these people.
- Focus on what you have, not what anyone else has.

We just explored how to deal with the fact that some people in your life will have more money than you do. Now let's flip the script. If you practice the smart money habits we've discussed in this book, chances are you will find yourself more affluent than many of your peers. That's great, but it can lead to feelings of guilt. In our final chapter, we'll discuss how to overcome those feelings so you can enjoy the wealth you earn.

# 26

# *Never Feel Guilty About Having Money*

My wife and I are friends with a married couple who became wealthy working for one of the Silicon Valley software giants. You've heard of this business and probably use its products, but we'll just call it "Tech Company." When they came into their fortune, which happened suddenly, this couple started receiving calls from family members asking for money. (Old finance joke: *Where there's a will, there's a relative.*) Our friends' first instinct was to say yes to every request. They gave away a lot. But they learned quickly that they didn't have enough money to give to everyone who asked.

Here's the plot twist. As generous as they've been, our friends have had to turn down relatives' and friends' requests for loans, demands for outright gifts (*the nerve of some people*), and "offers" to invest in exciting business ideas. Because they've said no, our friends have developed guilt about their money. They've told us many times that they feel terrible turning down these requests, but their guilt also shows up in less-obvious ways. For example, our friends now say they "Hit the Tech Company lottery." Guilt over getting rich has apparently twisted our friends' sense of reality. They've convinced themselves that they didn't earn their money; it just landed in their bank account, like they won the lottery.

What I learned speaking with Gordon Gunnell, a licensed marriage and family therapist based in Arizona, confirmed what I know about our friends: they're good, generous people. "Many of those with greater empathy may be inclined to experience a sense of guilt about having more than others. Correspondingly, they may feel a sense of unfairness. So they attempt to balance the scale. Paradoxically, the more they try to make things fair, the more unfairness they see."

Our friends shared their wealth with relatives and friends. That was their way of trying to increase fairness for the people they care about. But that generosity encouraged more money requests. Whenever our friends said no, they felt they were failing to right an unfair wrong—and that loaded them down with guilt. I don't want this to happen to you.

---

**Be generous when you can. It will make you feel great. But having more money than your peers does not obligate you to give it away to anyone.**

---

## Be Generous, but Not Obligated

Showing generosity is a beautiful act.

Because you're learning at a young age how to be smart with money, the chances are high that you're going to have more of it than the average person. You'll find many opportunities to share your wealth with people and causes you want to support. That's another gift money offers you: the ability to enjoy the rewarding feeling of being generous.

But giving away your money just to overcome feelings of guilt is a losing strategy. As Gordon Gunnell explained, trying to fix the unfairness you see around you will only expose you to more of that same unfairness. Earn a reputation for giving away lots of money, and you'll find more and more people asking for it. When you inevitably start turning down requests, you'll feel the guilt you were trying to avoid.

Besides, feeling guilty about having money is an unproductive emotion that won't do you or anyone else any good. If you stack up more money than your peers have, and you want to help them financially, here's a better idea.

## Life Hack: Share Something Better Than Money

There's an old saying: *Give a man a fish, and you feed him for a day. Teach a man to fish, and you feed him for a lifetime.*

Instead of just handing over cash to friends or family members, offer to teach them some of the life hacks you've learned for smart money management. Over time, that will be worth far more than whatever money you could loan or give them today.

## Life Hack: Remember That Your Money Is Your Money

Whatever your feelings are about sharing what you have—whether it's guilt or a genuine desire to be generous—remind yourself that it's your money. That means the decision about what to do with it is yours, too. Always remember that whatever money you've earned, you've *earned*.

Ever hear the saying, *There's no I in team*? Well, there's both a "me" and a "my" in money. And that's okay.

## Life Hack: Remember That Fairness Isn't Part of Nature

Here's one more great insight from Gordon Gunnell: "We need to recognize that fairness does not spontaneously occur anywhere in nature. It's a human construct. The healthiest way to live is to accept unfairness as a law of nature, focus on gratitude for what we have, and be generous when we can."

> **KEY TAKEAWAYS**
>
> - Generosity lets you do good in the world and feel great yourself. But use only those factors—and never guilt—when deciding whether to share your money.
> - Fairness isn't part of nature. The best we can do is to be grateful for what we have and be generous when we can.
> - Always remember that whatever money you've earned, you've *earned*.

# 27

# *Parting Thoughts*

## Money Is Just One Piece of Life's Puzzle

You made it to the end. Congratulations. That was no small task. And before we say goodbye, I'd like to leave you with one more thought.

We've talked so much about money in this book that I worry I've given you the impression it's the most important aspect of life. Money does play a role in many key areas of our lives, but it's those areas—not money itself—that really matter. Let's quickly review two examples.

Why do so many people fall into a Spending Rip Current and end up with Tomorrow's Junk? Often, it's because their brains are starving for engaging experiences and will look for them everywhere. If they don't have something constructive or creative to do with their time, these people often fall into a destructive pattern of passively consuming entertainment or scrolling social media. Either way, they'll be spending most of their time receiving advertisers' messages—some overt, some hidden. And that will almost certainly lead to mindless spending on stuff they don't need.

So there's one great reason (among many) to take up challenging hobbies. Learn another language. Start rock climbing. Teach yourself photography. Join a gym. In his great book *Flow*, psychology professor Mihalyi Csikszentmihalyi (*calm down, spell check*) explains that our brains crave what he describes as "optimal experiences."[1] You know this feeling. It's what happens when you're so immersed in an activity—a game, a sport, even a fun project in school or at work—that you lose yourself in what you're doing. You don't get hungry or thirsty. You don't need to use the bathroom. You lose track of time. Five hours can zoom by in what feels like a minute. If you can find some engrossing activities like these, you'll be spending so much time enjoying optimal-experience moments that you'll be too busy to browse retail websites or listen to the manipulative messages of advertisers.

Why do so many people spend money to keep up with peers? Often, it's because they want to ensure their place in a desired social circle. Remember what clinical psychologist Harriet Boxer told us back in the chapter on advertising: "How someone dresses, such as what brands of shoes or clothing they wear, can signal someone's status or affiliation with a group." The money itself isn't really important here. Neither are the clothes it buys. When you get down to the fundamental truth, we're all just trying to connect with a tribe, to be accepted into a group. The world can be a lonely place, and humans are social animals.

So here again, we find that money isn't what we're really after. We spend to keep up with our peers because we want these people to view us as one of them, to accept us into their tribe. But instead of spending yourself into debt just so you can buy the expensive things you think will earn you membership in some social group, you're better off spending your energy finding the right friends—friends who will accept you for more important qualities than how much money you have.

And where will you find those better friends? Maybe out rock climbing, or in the photography classes you're taking to keep your mind busy and yourself away from Amazon.com. Taking up interesting hobbies like these can also help you find and build friendships with like-minded people.

So, here's my bottom-line advice to you, the one big life hack I hope you'll take away from our conversation. Focus on what matters, what *really* matters: learning, growing, challenging your mind and body, building deep friendships, showing kindness, doing good in the world, and having fun. The money will come. And with the principles you've learned here, you'll be able to keep it and make it grow.

To your success!

# Notes

## Introduction

1. C. Horymski, "Average Credit Card Debt by Age in 2024," *Experian*, July 2, 2024. Available online: https://www.experian.com/blogs/ask-experian/research/credit-card-debt-by-age/.

2. CFPB Offices of Markets and Consumer Populations, "Overdraft/NSF Revenue in 2023 Down More than 50% Versus Pre-Pandemic Levels," *ConsumerFinance.gov*, April 24, 2024. Available online: https://www.consumerfinance.gov/data-research/research-reports/data-spotlight-overdraft-nsf-revenue-in-2023-down-more-than-50-versus-pre-pandemic-levels-saving-consumers-over-6-billion-annually/.

3. A. Solá, "37% of Americans Paid a Late Fee in the Last 12 Months, Report Finds," *CNBC*, May 30, 2024. Available online: https://www.cnbc.com/2024/05/30/37percent-of-americans-paid-a-late-fee-in-the-last-12-months-report-finds.html.

4. Federal Reserve, "Report on the Economic Well-Being of U.S. Households in 2022," *FederalReserve.gov*, May 2023. Available online: https://www.federalreserve.gov/publications/2023-economic-well-being-of-us-households-in-2022-expenses.htm.

## Chapter 1

1. Michael Schuman, *Will Smith: A Biography of a Rapper Turned Movie Star* (Enslow Publishers, 2013), 26.

2  E. Nelson, "Will Smith's Net Worth Is Fit for a Prince! How the Actor Earns Money Amid Gemini Man Lawsuit," *Yahoo! Entertainment*, September 4, 2024. Available online: https://www.yahoo.com/entertainment/smith-net-worth-fit-prince-171002289.html.

3  J. Taylor, "Exactly How Rich Is Will Smith? Here's What We Know About His Net Worth," *Men's Health*, October 11, 2019. Available online: https://www.menshealth.com/entertainment/a23006732/will-smith-net-worth/.

4  N. Dow, "More Than Half of Us Don't Keep a Budget or Know How Much We Spend," *The Penny Hoarder*, June 15, 2021. Available online: https://www.thepennyhoarder.com/budgeting/budgeting-statistics/.

# Chapter 2

1  K. Kelton, "Survey: Nearly Half of American Credit Cardholders Still Carry Debt, Many for at Least a Year," *Bankrate*, January 8, 2025. Available online: https://www.bankrate.com/credit-cards/news/credit-card-debt-survey/.

2  M. Schulz, "2025 Credit Card Debt Statistics," *LendingTree*, March 19, 2025. Available online: https://www.lendingtree.com/credit-cards/study/credit-card-debt-statistics/.

3  H. Hershfield, "A Lesson from FaceApp: Learning to Relate to the Older Person We Will Become," *The Los Angeles Times*, July 29, 2019. Available online: https://www.latimes.com/opinion/story/2019-07-26/hershfield-faceapp-relating-to-our-future-selves.

4  H. Hershfield, "A Lesson from FaceApp: Learning to Relate to the Older Person We Will Become," *The Los Angeles Times*, July 29, 2019. Available online: https://www.latimes.com/opinion/story/2019-07-26/hershfield-faceapp-relating-to-our-future-selves.

5  T. Barnes, "New Year's Resolutions: Why Do We Give Up on Them So Quickly?" *Baylor College of Medicine*, January 11, 2024. Available online: https://www.bcm.edu/news/new-years-resolutions-why-do-we-give-up-on-them-so-quickly.

6  Command Performance: Gilbert Gottfried, [One Night Stand TV program; Season 4, Episode 11] HBO, 1992.

# Chapter 3

1. R. Berger, "Top 100 Money Quotes of All Time," *Forbes*, April 30, 2014. Available online: https://www.forbes.com/sites/robertberger/2014/04/30/top-100-money-quotes-of-all-time/.

2. E. Martin, "Nicolas Cage Once Blew $150 Million on a Private Island and a Dinosaur Skull—Here's Everything He Bought," *CNBC*, January 20, 2018. Available online: https://www.cnbc.com/2018/01/19/how-nicholas-cage-once-blew-his-entire-150-million-fortune.html.

3. D. McAdam, "How Nicolas Cage Wildly Blew His Entire Fortune," *Yahoo! Finance*, June 20, 2024. Available online: https://uk.finance.yahoo.com/news/nicolas-cage-wildly-blew-entire-160000477.html.

4. National Ocean Service, "What Is a Rip Current?" *OceanService.NOAA.gov*, June 16, 2024. Available online: https://oceanservice.noaa.gov/facts/ripcurrent.html.

5. J. Walrack, "What Is Doom Spending and How Can You Avoid It?" *US News & World Report*, May 24, 2024. Available online: https://money.usnews.com/money/personal-finance/spending/articles/what-is-doom-spending-and-how-can-you-avoid-it.

6. J. Groopman, "Can Brain Science Help Us Break Bad Habits?" *The New Yorker*, October 21, 2019. Available online: https://www.newyorker.com/magazine/2019/10/28/can-brain-science-help-us-break-bad-habits.

7. S. Stosny, "Changing Emotional Habits," *Psychology Today*, October 13, 2019. Available online: https://www.psychologytoday.com/us/blog/anger-in-the-age-of-entitlement/201910/changing-emotional-habits.

8. E. Downing, "The Psychology of Spending," *Massachusetts Institute of Technology*, Winter 1999. Available online: https://betterworld.mit.edu/spectrum/issues/winter-1999/the-psychology-of-spending/.

9. National Ocean Service, "What Is a Rip Current?" *OceanService.NOAA.gov*, June 16, 2024. Available online: https://oceanservice.noaa.gov/facts/ripcurrent.html.

10. S. Stosny, "Changing Emotional Habits," *Psychology Today*, October 13, 2019. Available online: https://www.psychologytoday.com/us/blog/anger-in-the-age-of-entitlement/201910/changing-emotional-habits.

# Chapter 4

1. A. Tapper and S. Molas, "Midbrain Circuits of Novelty Processing," *Neurobiology of Learning and Memory* 176 (2020). Available online: https://pmc.ncbi.nlm.nih.gov/articles/PMC8091486/.

2. S. Springer, "Why Is it So Hard to Stop Buying More Stuff?" *Boston Globe*, May 18, 2017. Available online: https://www.bostonglobe.com/magazine/2017/05/18/why-hard-stop-buying-more-stuff/TikBKa6hUCSN2UkKoSBSeL/story.html.

3. J. Becker, "The Top 9 Expert Strategies to Declutter Your Home," *Forbes*, July 8, 2020. Available online: https://www.forbes.com/sites/joshuabecker/2020/07/08/the-top-9-expert-strategies-to-declutter-your-home/.

4. J. Feuer, "The Clutter Culture," *UCLA Magazine*, July 1, 2012. Available online: https://newsroom.ucla.edu/magazine/center-everyday-lives-families-suburban-america.

5. National Institute of Diabetes and Digestive and Kidney Diseases, "Cushing's Syndrome", *National Institutes of Health*, 2018. Available online: https://www.niddk.nih.gov/health-information/endocrine-diseases/cushings-syndrome.

# Chapter 5

1. Indiana University Bloomington, "Career Exploration & Student Employment." Available online: https://careerexploration.indiana.edu/career-guides/marketing-advertising-public-relations.html.

2. TIME Magazine Staff, "TIME 100 Persons of the Century," June 14, 1999. Available online: https://time.com/archive/6735625/time-100-persons-of-the-century/.

3. University of Southern California, Applied Sciences, "Thinking vs. Feeling: The Psychology of Advertising," November 17, 2023. Available online: https://appliedpsychologydegree.usc.edu/blog/thinking-vs-feeling-the-psychology-of-advertising.

4. Statista, "Advertising—United States," October, 2024. Available online: https://www.statista.com/outlook/amo/advertising/united-states.

## Chapter 6

1. Discover Card Smarts, "What is the Average Credit Card Debt in the United States?" November 19, 2024. Available online: https://www.discover.com/credit-cards/card-smarts/average-credit-card-debt/.

2. Federal Communications Commission, "Loud Commercials," September 24, 2021. Available online: https://www.fcc.gov/media/policy/loud-commercials.

## Chapter 7

1. *Rounders,* 1998, [Movie]: https://www.youtube.com/watch?v=5vEp5Bv-J40 &t=61s.

## Chapter 8

1. FBI: Famous Cases and Criminals, "Willie Sutton." Available online: https://www.fbi.gov/history/famous-cases/willie-sutton.

2. Bank of America, "Glossary of Banking Terms." Available online: https://www.bankofamerica.com/deposits/manage/glossary/.

3. M. Goldberg, "Checking Account Fees: What They Are and How to Avoid Them," *Bankrate*, October 14, 2024. Available online: https://www.bankrate.com/banking/checking/checking-account-fees/.

4. R. Bennett, "How Much Are ATM Fees?", *Bankrate*, February 28, 2025. Available online: https://www.bankrate.com/banking/how-much-are-atm-fees/.

## Chapter 9

1. Northwestern University, "Savings Accounts," Northwestern Money 101 Overview. Available online: https://www.northwestern.edu/financial-wellness/money-101/banking/savings-accounts.html.

2. Federal Reserve, "Report on the Economic Well-Being of U.S. Households in 2022," *FederalReserve.gov*, May 2023. Available online: https://www.federalreserve.gov/publications/2023-economic-well-being-of-us-households-in-2022-expenses.htm.

3. Morgan Housel, *The Psychology of Money* (Harriman House, 2020), 145.

# Chapter 10

1. M. Hoffman and T. Seychelle, "What Is a Credit Card?" *Bankrate*, September 4, 2024. Available online: https://www.bankrate.com/credit-cards/advice/what-is-a-credit-card/.

2. E. Downing, "The Psychology of Spending," Massachusetts Institute of Technology, Winter 1999. Available online: https://betterworld.mit.edu/spectrum/issues/winter-1999/the-psychology-of-spending/.

3. When Fighting Is Your Relationship's Default Setting, [TV program, Comedy Central Stand-Up] Comedy Central, 2013. Available online: https://www.youtube.com/watch?v=oUm3bETrXFw.

4. J. Caporal, "This Is How Credit Card Companies Hauled in $176 Billion in 2020," *The Motley Fool*, February 14, 2025. Available online: https://www.fool.com/money/research/credit-card-company-earnings/.

5. J. Caporal, "This Is How Credit Card Companies Hauled in $176 Billion in 2020," *The Motley Fool*, February 14, 2025. Available online: https://www.fool.com/money/research/credit-card-company-earnings/.

6. Federal Reserve, "Report on the Economic Well-Being of U.S. Households in 2022—May 2023," *FederalReserve.gov*, 2023. Available online: https://www.federalreserve.gov/publications/2023-economic-well-being-of-us-households-in-2022-expenses.htm.

7. Discover Card Smarts, "What is the Average Credit Card Debt in the United States?" November 19, 2024. Available online: https://www.discover.com/credit-cards/card-smarts/average-credit-card-debt/.

8. M. Schulz, "Average Credit Card Interest Rate in America Today," *LendingTree*, March 19, 2025. Available online: https://www.lendingtree.com/credit-cards/study/average-credit-card-interest-rate-in-america/.

9 Discover, "Credit Card Interest Calculator." Available online: https://www.discover.com/credit-cards/credit-card-calculator/credit-card-interest-calculator/.

10 Bill Bonner, *Hormegeddon: How Too Much of a Good Thing Leads to Disaster* (Lioncrest Publishing, 2014), 232.

11 J. Cazzin, "FP Explains: How Compound Interest Can Turn One Penny into Over $5 Million in 30 Days," *Financial Post*, May 28, 2021. Available online: https://financialpost.com/investing/fp-explains-heres-what-benjamin-franklin-can-teach-investors-about-compound-interest.

12 R. Downie, "This Is the 8th Wonder of the World, According to Albert Einstein. And Utilizing It Correctly Can Help Make Saving for Retirement an Absolute Breeze," *The Motley Fool*, March 16, 2024. Available online: https://www.fool.com/retirement/2024/03/16/this-is-the-8th-wonder-of-the-world-according-to-a/.

# Chapter 11

1 Equifax, "What Is a Credit Score?" Available online: https://www.equifax.com/personal/education/credit/score/articles/-/learn/what-is-a-credit-score/.

2 J. Akin, "What Affects Your Credit Scores?" *Experian*, July 29, 2023. Available online: https://www.experian.com/blogs/ask-experian/credit-education/score-basics/what-affects-your-credit-scores/.

3 Avengers: Age of Ultron, [Movie], TopMovieClips, 2015. Available online: https://youtu.be/PTbcaC0mGY8?si=4ZoouDBvnsEdH2_T.

4 Bad Credit, Dusty Slay [Video Clip provided by CDBaby], 2014. Available online: https://www.youtube.com/watch?v=ybiI6Bbe_dA.

5 Equifax, "How Are Credit Scores Calculated?" Available online: https://www.equifax.com/personal/education/credit/score/articles/-/learn/how-is-credit-score-calculated/.

## Chapter 12

1. D. Spector, "8 Banking Horror Stories That Will Outrage Consumers," *Business Insider*, December 21, 2011. Available online: https://www.businessinsider.com/banking-horror-stories-2011-12#tilmon-browns-daughter-ended-up-paying-71-for-fries-and-a-drink-6.

2. M. Burnette, "What Is a Debit Card and How Does It Work?" *NerdWallet*, February 3, 2025. Available online: https://www.nerdwallet.com/article/banking/what-is-a-debit-card.

3. CFPB Office of Research, "Overdraft and Nonsufficient Fund Fees: Insights from the Making Ends Meet Survey and Consumer Credit Panel," *ConsumerFinance.gov*, December 19, 2023. Available online: https://www.consumerfinance.gov/data-research/research-reports/overdraft-and-nonsufficient-fund-fees-insights-from-the-making-ends-meet-survey-and-consumer-credit-panel/.

4. J. Merritt, "Are Debit Cards Protected from Fraud?" *US News & World Report*, November 22, 2024. Available online: https://www.usnews.com/banking/articles/are-debit-cards-protected-from-fraud.

## Chapter 13

1. Jerry Seinfeld, [Video clip, The Late Show with David Letterman], 1989. Available online: https://www.youtube.com/watch?v=LSZsDZ0k5AE.

2. L. Fruen, "SO LITTLE TIME: Americans Will Spend More than Five Years of Their Lives Doing Tasks They Hate, Study Finds," *The US Sun*, June 17, 2021. Available online: https://www.the-sun.com/news/3105446/americans-spend-five-years-tasks-they-hate/.

3. Cambridge Dictionary, "Bill." https://dictionary.cambridge.org/us/dictionary/english/bill.

4. A. Solá, "37 percent of Americans Paid a Late Fee in the Last 12 Months, Report Finds," *CNBC*, May 30, 2024. Available online: https://www.cnbc.com/2024/05/30/37percent-of-americans-paid-a-late-fee-in-the-last-12-months-report-finds.html.

# Chapter 14

1. Seinfeld: The Alternate Side, [TV show; Season 3, Episode 11], NBC, 1991. Available online: https://youtu.be/4T2GmGSNvaM?si=WMUbtmbL3E3J7QhD.

2. K. Bennett, "The Average American Household Budget," *Bankrate*, December 10, 2024. Available online: https://www.bankrate.com/banking/savings/average-household-budget/.

3. A. Marder, "Most Americans Have a Monthly Budget, but Many Still Overspend," *NerdWallet*, May 30, 2023. Available online: https://www.nerdwallet.com/article/finance/data-2023-budgeting-report.

4. Chatterton & Associates, "7 Signs You Should Talk to a Certified Financial Planner," 2023. Available online: https://chattertoninc.com/blog/7-signs-you-should-talk-to-a-certified-financial-plannertm.

5. Financial Literacy: Managing Your Money at Yale, "Budgeting and Goal Setting," Yale University. Available online: https://finlit.yale.edu/planning/budgeting-and-goal-setting.

6. David Bach, *The Latte Factor* (Simon & Schuster, 2019), 51.

# Chapter 15

1. Axis Max Life Insurance, "What Is Investment?" Available online: https://www.maxlifeinsurance.com/blog/investments/what-is-investment.

2. The Bahnsen Group, "Principles." Available online: https://thebahnsengroup.com/principles/.

3. D. Green, "Eight Great Investing Quotes," *Wells Fargo*. Available online: https://fa.wellsfargoadvisors.com/DavidCGreen/Eight-Great-Investing-Quotes.c10271.htm.

4. J. Maverick, "S&P 500 Average Returns and Historical Performance," *Investopedia*, December 26, 2024. Available online: https://www.investopedia.com/ask/answers/042415/what-average-annual-return-sp-500.asp.

5. Morgan Housel, *The Psychology of Money* (Harriman House, 2020), 53.

## Chapter 16

1. M. Lungariello, "Bank Robbery Foiled When Teller Can't Read Stickup Note," *New York Post*, August 12, 2021. Available online: https://nypost.com/2021/08/12/bank-robbery-foiled-when-teller-cant-read-stickup-note/.

2. S. Silverman, "Kevin Bacon Admits He Lost Most of His Net Worth to Bernie Madoff's Too Good to Be True Ponzi Scheme," *Entrepreneur*, October 11, 2022. Available online: https://www.entrepreneur.com/business-news/how-much-money-did-kevin-bacon-lose-to-bernie-madoff/437025.

3. S. Silverman, "Kevin Bacon Admits He Lost Most of His Net Worth to Bernie Madoff's Too Good to Be True Ponzi Scheme," *Entrepreneur*, October 11, 2022. Available online: https://www.entrepreneur.com/business-news/how-much-money-did-kevin-bacon-lose-to-bernie-madoff/437025.

4. A. Cullins, "Johnny Depp: A Star in Crisis and the Insane Story of His Missing Millions," *The Hollywood Reporter*, May 17, 2017. Available online: https://www.hollywoodreporter.com/movies/movie-features/johnny-depp-a-star-crisis-insane-story-his-missing-millions-1001513/.

5. N. Dillon, "Lindsay Lohan's Bank Accounts Seized by IRS in Effort to Recover Over $230K in Unpaid Taxes: Report," *New York Daily News*, January 10, 2019. Available online: https://www.nydailynews.com/2012/12/03/lindsay-lohans-bank-accounts-seized-by-irs-in-effort-to-recover-over-230k-in-unpaid-taxes-report/.

6. A. Neil, "Lindsay Lohan: How I Blew $30 Million," *Yahoo! Lifestyle*, October 27, 2010. Available online: https://au.lifestyle.yahoo.com/lindsay-lohan-blew-30-million-024644371.html.

## Chapter 17

1. Bread Financial, "From Friends to Foes: Money Ruins 1 in 5 Friendships," May 28, 2024. Available online: https://newsroom.breadfinancial.com/from-friends-to-foes-financial-incompatibility-study.

2. Bread Financial, "From Friends to Foes: Money Ruins 1 in 5 Friendships," May 28, 2024. Available online: https://newsroom.breadfinancial.com/from-friends-to-foes-financial-incompatibility-study.

# Chapter 19

1. D. Albert, J. Chein, and L. Steinberg, "The Teenage Brain: Peer Influences on Adolescent Decision Making," *Current Directions in Psychological Science* 22, no. 2 (2013). https://journals.sagepub.com/doi/full/10.1177/0963721412471347.

2. A. LeBaron-Black, H. Kelley, E. Hill, B. Jorgensen, and J. Jensen, "Financial Socialization Agents and Spending Behavior of Emerging Adults: Do Parents, Peers, Employment, and Media Matter?" *Journal of Financial Counseling and Planning* 34, no. 1 (2023): 6–19. https://files.eric.ed.gov/fulltext/EJ1383278.pdf.

3. C. Horymski, "Average Credit Card Debt by Age in 2024," *Experian*, July 2, 2024. Available online: https://www.experian.com/blogs/ask-experian/research/credit-card-debt-by-age/.

# Chapter 21

1. T. Schmall, "Neighbors Spend Thousands to Have Nicest House on the Block," *New York Post*, July 12, 2018. Available online: https://nypost.com/2018/07/12/neighbors-spend-thousands-to-have-nicest-house-on-the-block/.

2. D. Bates, "The 2 Faces of Social Comparison," *Psychology Today*, September 22, 2024. Available online: https://www.psychologytoday.com/us/blog/mental-health-nerd/202409/the-2-faces-of-social-comparison.

3. S. Agarwal, V. Mikhed, and B. Scholnick, "Peers' Income and Financial Distress: Evidence from Lottery Winners and Neighboring Bankruptcies," *Federal Reserve Bank of Philadelphia*, 2018, WP 18–22. Available online: https://www.philadelphiafed.org/-/media/FRBP/Assets/working-papers/2018/wp18-22.pdf?sc_lang=en.

4. S. Louis, "That Money Ain't Gonna Last Forever: NBA Legend Charles Barkley Reveals Why Nearly 80 percent of Professional Athletes Go Broke After Retirement—How to Avoid Their Wealth-Killing Mistakes," *MSN.com*, June 29, 2024. Available online: https://www.msn.com/en-us/sports/nba/that-money-aint-gonna-last-forever-nba-legend-charles-barkley-reveals-why

-nearly-80-of-professional-athletes-go-broke-after-retirement-how-to-avoid-their-wealth-killing-mistakes/ar-BB1p6LR9.

5  P. Torre, "How (and Why) Athletes Go Broke," *Sports Illustrated*, March 23, 2009. Available online: https://vault.si.com/vault/2009/03/23/how-and-why-athletes-go-broke.

## Chapter 22

1  E. Issa, "Survey: 54% Who Feel Money Envy Say It Harms Their Mental Health," *NerdWallet*, July 11, 2023. Available online: https://www.nerdwallet.com/article/finance/survey-money-envy-is-common-and-54-who-feel-it-say-it-harms-their-mental-health.

2  Discover Card Smarts, "What is the Average Credit Card Debt in the United States?" November 19, 2024. Available online: https://www.discover.com/credit-cards/card-smarts/average-credit-card-debt/.

3  E. Issa, "Survey: 54% Who Feel Money Envy Say It Harms Their Mental Health," *NerdWallet*, July 11, 2013. Available online: https://www.nerdwallet.com/article/finance/survey-money-envy-is-common-and-54-who-feel-it-say-it-harms-their-mental-health.

4  C. Rubin, "Who Says Money Can't Buy Happiness?" *Inc.com*, June 22, 2023. Available online: https://www.inc.com/news/articles/2010/09/study-says-75000-can-buy-happiness.html.

## Chapter 27

1  Mihaly Csikszentmihalyi, *Flow: The Psychology of Optimal Experience* (Harper Perennial, 1991), 3.

# Suggested Reading

## Personal Finance Strategies

*The Millionaire Next Door: The Surprising Secrets of America's Wealthy*
  Thomas J. Stanley and William D. Danko (Taylor Trade Publishing, 1996)
*The Total Money Makeover: A Proven Plan for Financial Fitness*
  Dave Ramsey (Thomas Nelson, 2003)

## How Money Works

*Basic Economics: A Citizen's Guide to the Economy*
  Thomas Sowell (Basic Books, 2000)
*There's No Free Lunch: 250 Economic Truths*
  David Bahnsen (Post Hill Press, 2021)

## Money and Happiness (and Why They're Often Very Different Things)

*The Psychology of Money: Timeless Lessons on Wealth, Greed, and Happiness*
  Morgan Housel (Harriman House, 2020)
*Flow: The Psychology of Optimal Experience*
  Mihaly Csikszentmihalyi (Harper Perennial Modern Classics, 2008)
*The Practicing Stoic: A Philosophical User's Manual*
  Ward Farnsworth (David R. Godine Publishing, 2018)

## Understanding Advertising

*Confessions of an Advertising Man*
    David Ogilvy (Vintage, 1985)
*Positioning: The Battle for Your Mind*
    Al Ries and Jack Trout (McGraw Hill, 2000)

## Investing Fundamentals

*Most Important Thing*
    Howard Marks (Harper Collins, 2018)
*The Intelligent Investor*
    Benjamin Graham (Harper Business, 2006)

# Index

Ad Barrage 50
    ad influence awareness 42–5
    advertising manipulation
        awareness 47–8
    early adopter 45–6
    follower 46
    purchase decision reasoning 47
advertisers 41, 43, 45–7, 58, 194.
    *See also* Ad Barrage
Aerial View
    advertisers grabbing
        attention 52
    evaluating purchase habits 54
    finding gratification in smart
        choices 54–5
    identifying spending
        patterns 49–50
    psychological and biological
        triggers 50–1
    rip current perspective 53–4
Amazon.com 195
AnnualCreditReport.com 100
automated teller machine (ATM)
    card 69, 70, 74, 103

Bach, David 117
Bacon, Kevin 132
Bahnsen, David 124
The Bahnsen Group 124

balance 3, 82, 89, 190
Bankrate.com 69, 81
Bates, Dan 161
being real 179–80
    avoiding illusions 182
    bad outcomes 180–1
    true friends 181–2
bill 107, 134
    automate bill payments 110
    bill-paying responsibility
        109–10
    creating calendar event 110–12
    defined 108
billing cycle 83
Bonner, Bill 89
borrowing money 145–6
    can't-miss reminder 147
    repay promptly 148
    types of borrowing from
        friends 146–7
Boxer, Harriet 46, 194
budgets 114
    automate payments 117–18
    envelope method 117
    gamifying budgets 118
    proportional budgeting 117
    traditional method 116
    writing budget with magic 115
Burnett, Leo 41, 42, 45

Cage, Nicolas  25, 36
cash out  127
certificate of deposit (CD)  75
charitable giving  154
checking account  65, 73, 74
   benefits  68-9
   defined  66
   managing  67-8
   monitoring account
      frequently  71-2
   risks of misuse  69-70
   setting low-balance alerts  71
   setting payment alerts  70-1
   working  67
Commercial Advertisement
   Loudness Mitigation (CALM)
   Act  52
compounding  73, 89, 126
compound interest  89
convenience  4, 85, 87
Crapper, Thomas  166
credit, defined  97
credit card  1-4, 28-9, 81-3, 146
   business model  84-5
   compounding interest  89
   outstanding balance  85-6
   paying bill in full & early  90
   risks and pitfalls  87-9
   smart use  86-7
   working  83-4
credit report  94-6, 104
credit score  81
   avoiding excess credit  99
   defined  93-4
   finance quirks  94-5
   good score range  99
   importance  95-7
   keeping accounts active  99
   monitoring scores regularly  100
   secrets to high score  97-9
Csikszentmihalyi, Mihalyi  194

Days Without Spending  59, 60
debit card  65
   benefits  103
   build a cushion  105
   defined  102
   fees overview  101-2
   mismanaging risks  103-5
   monitoring accounts  105-6
debt, defined  97
decluttering  36
   movement  38
delaying gratification  55
demand deposit accounts  66, 74
Depp, Johnny  133
digital coin  125
Discover Card  88
doom spending  27
dopamine  36, 151

Einstein, Albert  89
endorphins  15, 27, 28, 31, 36, 39, 102, 151
Equifax  93, 97

fairness  190, 192
Federal Reserve  88
Federal Reserve Bank of
   Philadelphia  163
*Flow* (Csikszentmihalyi)  193
Franklin, Benjamin  89
future self  21

gambling  123, 124
Gamify Your Money Habits
   retail traps  61
   strategies  58-61
Generation Z  2
generosity  185, 190
giving plan  154
   adding donations to budget  157
   charity check  156

## Index

donation request 154–5
ideas 155–6
standard phrase 156–7
Gottfried, Gilbert 22
guilt feelings 189–90
fairness 192
money you've earned, you've earned 191–2
sharing something better than money 191
showing generosity 190–1
Gunnell, Gordon 190–2

habit 27, 28, 35
habituation 33
healthy new habit 31
Hershfield, Hal 21
home improvements 159
Housel, Morgan 76, 126
human history 161
human nature 124, 160, 167
Hyman, Rita 61

inflation 77, 126
installment loans 98
interchange fees 86
interest 3, 4, 74, 82, 85
interest fees 85
interest rate 3, 88, 93
investments 73
benefits 125–7
defined 122
investment opportunity 127–8
invest thoughtfully and patiently 124–5
keeping it boring 129
logic 123–4
investment success 125, 129
Investopedia 125, 126

jealousy 169
being grateful and celebrate their success 171
counting other people's money 171–2
strategies 170
Jost, Colin 84

Last Year Me 23
late fee 4, 109
*The Latte Factor* (Bach) 117
lending 3, 74
lending policy 139
ground rules 143–4
no-lending phrase 142–3
no-lending policy 141–2
reasons 140
risks 140–1
Lohan, Lindsay 134
low-balance alert 71

Madoff, Bernie 132
Markell, Jerry 20, 126, 182
Martin, Steve 25
minimum balance 74, 75
minimum payment 3, 83, 88
Monday Me 6, 17, 19, 31, 38, 39, 49, 51, 85, 87, 127
facing facts 21–2
gifting to future you 23
Next Week Me 20–1
using age-imaging app 23–4
money as competition
being honest about spending 165–6
game with no winners 164
hopeless romantic 162
keeping up with peers 162–4
picturing royals 166
real friends 165
social comparison dangers 161

money privacy
    avoid sharing specific numbers   175
    choosing preferences wisely   176
    Social Security Number   173–5
    standard phrase   175–6
Money Toolkit   7, 73, 103, 106, 132, 134
    just-in-case savings cushion   133
    pay bills early   134
    shortcuts with investments   132

National Association of Productivity and Organizing Professionals   36
National Ocean Service   26, 29
NerdWallet   102
Next Month Me   20, 22, 23
Next Year Me   22, 23
no-lending policy   142
nonprofit organizations   153
non-sufficient funds   104

optimal experiences   194
other people's money
    imagining roles reversed   186
    legitimate reasons not to give money   184–6
    more money, more problems   184
outstanding balance   83, 85, 88
overdraft charges   4, 69, 71, 75, 104

Patel, Raj   13, 15, 27, 52, 162
paycheck   66, 78
PayPal   68
peer pressure
    choosing peers wisely   152
    having standard phrase   151–2
    positive or resisted   150–1
personal finance   3, 5

personal identification number (PIN)   102
personal loans   141
*Positioning: The Battle for Your Mind* (Trout and Ries)   47
product placement   43, 59
psychographics (in advertising)   45
*The Psychology of Money* (Housel)   76, 126
*Psychology Today* (Stosny)   28, 29, 161

retail therapy   15
revolving loan   98
Right Now Me   39
*Rounders* (1998)   57

Samuelson, Paul   125
savings account   73–5, 127, 161
    benefits   75–6
    drawback   76–7
    gamify savings   77
    high-interest account   78
    same bank advantage   78
Sedgwick, Kyra   132
Seinfeld, Jerry   107, 113
Slay, Dusty   97
smart money management   4–6, 48, 115, 191
smart spending habits   48
Smith, Will   11–14, 16, 133
social comparison   161, 166, 169
social media   7, 19, 128, 161, 162
Social Security Number   173
Spending Rip Current   6, 24, 50, 51, 103, 108, 126, 193
    beach scene   26
    credit cards   28–9
    emotional triggers   27
    habit formation   27–8
    lifeguard   29

new habit  29–31
swimming sideways  31
*Sports Illustrated*  163
Stosny, Steven  28, 30, 58
strategic giving plan  155, 156
Strickland, Erick  163
Summertime Me  20
Sutton, Willie  65, 66

Taylor  160, 161
time deposit account  74, 75
*TIME Magazine*  41
Today Me  53, 102
Tomorrow's Junk  34, 50, 54, 102, 108, 115, 126, 181
   brain's craving for novelty  35–6
   decluttering  36–8
   in-home treadmill  34–5

making Tomorrow Me earn it  39
saving item to cart  38–9
Townes, Jeff  11

UCLA study  21, 23, 38
US Department of Education  150

Venmo  65, 69

Whole Money Picture  20, 24, 49, 53, 69, 70, 78, 86, 105, 108, 114, 155, 157
   endorphins  14–15
   playing game  12–14
   sport nor therapy  16–17
   tracking  15–16

Zelle  67, 68, 143

# About the Author

**Robbie Hyman** is a marketing copywriter who has been helping businesses tell their stories for more than twenty years. While he still struggles to fix even the simplest issues with his computer or phone, multibillion-dollar Silicon Valley giants—and tech companies across the United States, Canada, Europe, and Israel—consistently turn to him for clear, compelling marketing content. Robbie is also a longtime contributing writer for publications like *LifeHack.org* and *Fedsmith.com*, where his articles have received millions of views. He lives in Phoenix with his very patient wife and daughter.